Helen's
Asian
Kitchen™

easy
asian
noodles

Helen's Asian Kitchen®

easy asian noodles

helen chen

photography by jason wyche

WILEY

JOHN WILEY & SONS, INC.

Published by John Wiley & Sons, Inc., Hoboken, New Jersey
Published simultaneously in Canada

Food styling by Jamie Kimm
Prop styling by Leslie Siegel

Library of Congress Cataloging-in-Publication Data
Chen, Helen.
  Helen's Asian kitchen: easy Asian noodles / Helen Chen; photography by Jason Wyche.
     p. cm.
  Includes index.
  ISBN 978-0-470-38755-9 (cloth)
  1. Cookery, Asian. 2. Cookery (Pasta) I. Title.
  TX724.5.A1C46 2010
  641.595--dc22
                          2008055997
Printed in China
10 9 8 7 6 5 4 3 2 1

To my husband, Keith, for holding up more than his share of the sky.

contents

acknowledgments

While working on this book, I was constantly reminded of the people, places, and events that influenced and enriched my culinary persona. Most significant were my mother and father. My mother, Joyce Chen, who not only taught me how to cook, but also nurtured my love of the foods and culture of China and the cooking experience itself. My father, Thomas Chen, whose passion for good food was infectious. The years working alongside my parents and brothers at our family restaurant in Cambridge, Massachusetts, taught me at an early age the value of hard work, and also exposed me to all regions of Chinese cuisine. Multiple trips to Asia for business and pleasure, especially our first trip to the People's Republic of China in 1972, and getting to know our large extended family there. And, now my latest venture, after the sale of the family cookware business, is "Helen's Asian Kitchen," my eponymous line of Asian kitchenware.

I wish to thank the following for their supportive roles in the writing and production of this book:

To Barry Lockard, longtime friend and fellow cook, whose passion for food and proper English were indispensable.

To Tami Buhr and Jeff Gray, who, as my "tasters," provided honest opinions and were always eager to sample any kind of noodle.

To Hitomi Ohishi, my friend in Tokyo, Japan, for sharing her knowledge of Japanese noodles.

A special thanks to my goddaughter, Sophie Yang, and her husband, Allan Chen, for their support, and invaluable help with everything from computer glitches to tasting noodle dishes to translating Chinese packaging. And to their daughter, five-year-old Danielle, for making me laugh and loving to eat at Nai Nai's house.

To my agent, Judith Weber, for her professional guidance and for bringing me to John Wiley & Sons. And to my editor, Justin Schwartz, who skillfully and patiently guided me through the intricacies of the manuscript-to-published-book process. To Jason Wyche, for bringing my recipes to life in beautiful living color.

To Robert Laub for his friendship, support, and belief in my talents, resulting in Helen's Asian Kitchen®, the line of Asian kitchenware we created together.

To my family for their unconditional love and encouragement.

And last but not least, to my husband and partner in life, Keith Ohmart, for his devotion and companionship, patience, wise counsel, unending loyalty, and, in this particular case, for enduring nothing but noodles for months.

introduction

I've always joked with my Italian-American sister-in-law, Barbara, that pasta originally came from China to Italy via Marco Polo. Apocryphal or not, noodles have long been and still remain a major staple in Asian cuisine. Whether they're stir-fried, boiled, pan-fried, served in soup, or tossed with a sauce, they can be enjoyed anytime throughout the day—for breakfast, lunch, a light dinner, or a midnight snack. For most Asians, noodles conjure up thoughts of home, comfort, and good food.

different kinds of asian noodles

There are a myriad of different types of noodles enjoyed in Asia. The majority are made from either wheat or rice flour, but there are also noodles made from other ingredients such as mung beans, buckwheat, and potatoes. The noodles may be flat or round, wide or thin, fresh or dried, but unlike Italian pasta shapes, which are also sometimes short and stubby, almost all Asian noodles are long. This is probably because in many Asian cultures, noodles represent long life and are always served at birthdays and other celebratory occasions.

In the North, the noodles are commonly made of wheat flour because the cold, dry climate of northern Asia is not conducive to growing rice. In the South, the hot and wet climate does not allow for wheat crops, so they grow rice instead. In general the noodles eaten in the north versus south reflect this climatic difference. Therefore, noodle dishes from the north, such as Beijing, China, use wheat noodles, and the noodle dishes from the south, such as Vietnam and Thailand, use rice noodles.

Northern Chinese are famous for their hand-pulled or stretched noodles, known as *la mian*, translated as pulled (*la*) noodles (*mian*). A wad of dough is miraculously transformed into all kinds of noodles—flat, round, thick, thin, and the incredibly wispy Dragon's Beard noodles by repeatedly pulling, folding, twisting, and stretching the dough until the desired size is reached. A rolling pin is never used, just strength and dexterity. My mother told me that it took a special *gong fu* or inner strength and skill to accomplish this task.

I like to use good-quality dried noodles more often than fresh noodles because of their convenience, wide availability, long shelf life, and chewy texture. Many Asian noodles are interchangeable with Italian pasta. Keep in mind the original noodle size and shape as you choose a substitute. In general, I find the overall best substitute to be Italian vermicelli, thin spaghetti, or spaghettini. There isn't an acceptable substitute for the rice noodles, but many well-stocked supermarkets carry both wide and thin rice noodles in their ethnic section.

glossary of asian noodles

bean thread

Also known as cellophane or glass noodles, these wiry noodles are sold dried in 1-ounce bundles. They are made from the starch of mung beans, also known as green beans to the Chinese, and cook up clear, hence the names. Mung beans, when sprouted, give us the popular bean sprouts. These noodles are tasteless and therefore rarely cooked alone, but used as an ingredient in soup, stir fries, salads, or in fillings absorbing the flavors of the ingredients with which they are cooked. The noodles must be soaked in hot water for about 5 minutes until soft and translucent. Use scissors to cut them to more manageable lengths after they are soaked. Dry bean thread may also be deep fried for crisp fluffy noodles used to garnish dishes such as salads.

chinese egg noodles

Made from wheat flour, egg, and water, the yellow color of these noodles is best if it comes from the egg yolks and not from food coloring, so check the manufacturer's label. Available fresh or dried and in different widths, these noodles have a wonderful elastic, chewy texture and are excellent in stir-fried or pan-fried noodle dishes. The dried noodles are packaged in nest-like bundles and are also available flavored with shrimp, scallop, or crab. Fresh egg noodles come in plastic bags and will keep about one week in the refrigerator. Egg or wheat noodles may be used interchangeably. Cook fresh egg noodles in boiling water for 2 to 3 minutes, dried noodles for 3 to 4 minutes. Taste the noodles often while cooking to be sure they don't overcook and lose their nice chewy texture.

chinese wheat noodles

Made from wheat flour, water, and a little salt, these noodles play a large part in the Asian noodle repertoire. They are very versatile, have a nice resilient texture, hold up well to all kinds of cooking styles, and are available fresh or dried and in many different thicknesses and widths. Asian markets usually carry a few varieties of fresh wheat noodles, but dried varieties have a much longer shelf life and are more widely available. Dried wheat noodles can be found in boxes or wound into individual bundles. Both fresh and dried varieties cook rapidly and must be rinsed in cold water after cooking to remove the excess starch that can make them gummy. Cook fresh wheat noodles about 2 to 3 minutes, depending upon size. Dried noodles take only 3 to 5 minutes.

ramen or instant noodles

Most people are familiar with this ubiquitous noodle from the instant soup noodles found in most supermarkets. These Chinese-style egg noodles are actually pre-cooked, sometimes fried, then dried and packed into single-serving pouches with soup powder. Instant noodles are eaten by millions of Asians and have become a staple for a quick and inexpensive lunch. When I'm rushed I sometimes resort to instant ramen noodles myself, but always enrich the meal with chopped vegetables and maybe an egg poached in the broth.

Ramen noodles also come packaged in larger blocks without flavoring packets. In Japan, instant noodles are called *chuka soba*, which means "Chinese noodles." Cook instant noodles in boiling water for about 2 minutes. Be careful; they overcook easily.

rice noodles

 These noodles are made from rice flour and water and are more readily available dried than fresh. Rice noodles are more delicate than wheat noodles, especially the fine variety, and because they are very absorbent they tend to overcook easily. Overcooked rice noodles end up sticky and mushy.

There is a wide variety of rice noodles and as with many other Asian ingredients the nomenclature is not standard. Luckily, rice noodles are usually packaged in clear cellophane so it's better to rely on what they look like rather than the particular name used by the manufacturer.

Thin, round rice noodles are known as *pho* (extra fine rice noodles are known as *bun*) to the Vietnamese; rice sticks, rice vermicelli are called *mi fen* in Mandarin or *mai fun* in Cantonese to the Chinese. To the Thai, the wide, flat rice noodle used in such dishes as the popular Pad Thai, is known as *jantaboon*. The flat rice noodles are available in various widths—small (⅛-inch wide), medium (³⁄₁₆-inch wide), large (¼-inch wide), and extra-large (⅜-inch wide).

To give a better idea of the sizes, rice vermicelli or rice sticks resemble Italian vermicelli, the small flat rice noodle is equivalent in size to linguine, and the large flat rice noodle is like fettuccine.

I prefer to soak the thin rice noodles first in hot, not boiling, tap water until the strands separate and become flexible. This will take about 8 to 10 minutes, depending on how hot the water is. They are often cooked again either in a hot broth or stir-fried where the moisture from the ingredients they are cooked with will soften them further, so keeping them a little firmer will ensure a better textured final result at the end. Thin rice noodles that will be used cold in salads will have their texture improved if, after soaking, they are plunged in boiling water for a couple of minutes just to tenderize, then drained, rinsed in cold water, and allowed to drain again. Dry rice sticks may also be fried in hot oil for use in salads or as a garnish. Wide rice noodles, because of their thickness, require a little longer cooking time and should be boiled for about 3 to 5 minutes.

Don't confuse rice vermicelli with bean thread noodles. They may look similar when dried, but are very different when cooked. Look for "rice" in the ingredients. If it says "bean," then you have the wrong noodles.

Fresh Chinese rice sheets, known as *he fen* in Mandarin or *chow fun* in Cantonese, which translates as stir fry (*chow*) rice noodles (*fun*), are difficult to find and very perishable. So unless you have a very good, well-stocked Chinese market nearby, I find that extra-wide dried Thai rice noodles substitute beautifully.

soba noodles

A Japanese favorite, these noodles are made of wheat and buckwheat flours and water. The color may range from light brown to light green with the addition of *matcha*, Japanese green tea powder. A famous Japanese dish is a cold summertime specialty called *zaru soba*. Soba is sold dried, elegantly tied into small, 2-ounce bundles and packaged. Cook dried soba in boiling water for 5 to 6 minutes.

somen noodles

A very fine, thin, white Japanese noodle made with wheat flour and oil. They are neatly banded into single-portion bundles. Thin and delicate like angel hair pasta, these noodles are perfect for soups and in the summer are traditionally served over ice with a savory dipping sauce. Less common and more expensive are pastel-colored somen noodles that take on the color of added ingredients like egg (yellow), plum (pink), or green tea (green). The cooking time is very brief—only about 2 minutes.

udon noodles

These hearty, thick Japanese wheat noodles can be found either round or flat. They form the basis of many delicious noodle dishes—mainly soups and stir-fries. I remember being mesmerized at one Japanese noodle shop that had a chef making hand-rolled udon noodles in the store window, enticing diners into their establishment. Because of their thickness, it takes 10 to 12 minutes to cook dried udon noodles and only 2 to 3 minutes for the fresh variety.

wonton skins

Although not actually a noodle, wonton wrappers are made from the same flour-water dough from which noodles come. Wrapped wontons are often served alone, in clear soup or with noodles in soup, a Hong Kong specialty. They serve the same gustatory function as noodles. The square skins are widely available in supermarkets.

serving and eating asian soup noodles

In Asia, noodles, especially soup noodles, are commonly enjoyed as a light meal or healthy snack. Stir-fried or pan-fried noodle dishes may also be served this way or as part of a multi-course meal. Some of the heartier noodle dishes cooked with meat or seafood and vegetables may also serve as a complete one-dish meal. Some others are best served as a side dish. Most of the recipes in this book serve 4 people, allowing 2 to 3 ounces of noodles per person. If you want a more substantial meal, plan on each recipe serving 3 people.

I find that Westerners are not always familiar with the way Asian soup noodles should be served. First, the Asian noodle bowl is a rather large affair—something akin to a small mixing bowl with at least a 4-cup capacity. It has to be deep enough to accommodate not only the noodles and the soup, but also any ingredients that accompany it. Having large, deep bowls is essential for the proper presentation and enjoyment of these noodles.

Forks are useless table implements for picking up long, slippery soup noodles. I'll never forget the lunch of soup noodles I made for my mother-in-law and two of her friends, neither of whom were Asian. They couldn't handle chopsticks well, so attempted to eat the noodles with forks. It was impossible and I felt so badly watching them struggle as the noodles constantly slipped off their forks. If possible, provide chopsticks and soup spoons, or if that won't work, provide a fork and spoon so the noodles can be twirled on the spoon.

cooking the noodles

How long to boil the noodles is determined by whether they are dried or fresh, thick or thin, made from wheat or rice, or are the pre-cooked instant variety. It's a good idea to test a few strands often for doneness as they are cooking. They should be a little softer than al dente. But keep in mind that many of the noodle recipes call for the noodles to be cooked again, so veer on the firm side if unsure.

The rule of thumb on cooking noodles, whether fresh or dried, is always to use enough boiling water so the noodles will cook evenly and have plenty of room to expand. Once the noodles are in the water and the water has returned to a boil, the heat may be turned down just to maintain a constant boil. This will help prevent boil-overs. Be sure to stir the noodles occasionally for even cooking and to prevent them from sticking to one another. This is especially important for the dried noodle bundles. There is no need to salt or add oil to the boiling water. Be vigilant with the cooking time, especially with fresh noodles that cook in just a few minutes. Do not overcook or allow the noodles to sit in hot water after they are cooked. The noodles will absorb too much water and become soggy and lose their "bite." In general, Asian-style wheat noodles cook faster than dried Italian-style pasta. Finally, Asians like to rinse the noodles in cold water after cooking to remove any excess starch. This makes the noodles smooth and chewy.

The Japanese cook their noodles a little differently. When the water is at a rolling boil, the noodles are added and gently stirred to prevent sticking. When the water returns to a boil, a cup of cold water is added and the water is allowed to return to a boil. Some people like to repeat this step a second time before letting the noodles finish cooking. I find that this technique does help to avoid messy boil-overs, especially since Japanese noodles tend to create more foam in the water. It isn't necessary to cook Japanese noodles this way, but if not, watch to keep the water from boiling over.

Because Asians rinse the noodles after cooking, the noodles must be reheated briefly when they are served in a hot broth so as not to cool down the soup too much. The reheating process also loosens the noodles so they can be easily distributed into individual serving bowls.

Restaurants and professional chefs reheat and loosen pre-cooked noodles by putting them in special deep and narrow wire baskets with long vertical handles. The baskets are dipped into a large vat of boiling water or stock, drained, and quickly transferred to a bowl, whereupon sauce or hot broth is poured over the noodles, garnished, and served immediately.

This method is not always practical at home. Instead of draining the boiling water in which the noodles were cooked, you can strain the noodles out of the water with chopsticks or tongs and reserve the boiling water in the pot to reheat the noodles later. Or, you can drain the noodles in a colander placed over another pot so the boiling water will be retained. These two methods will help avoid having to boil another pot of water to reheat the noodles. A third method is to rinse the cooked noodles with a kettle of boiling water or very hot tap water just before use.

Drained noodles quickly become compact. To make them easier to handle for stir-frying, lightly rinse or sprinkle the noodles with a few tablespoons of tap water and then loosen and fluff with your fingers before adding them to the pan. I prefer this method over oiling the noodles because it helps to cut down on the total amount of oil used.

tools for the asian kitchen

wok or stir-fry pan

For stir-frying noodles, I prefer to use either a 14-inch diameter non-stick flat-bottom wok or a stir-fry pan. Skillets and frying pans with their low sides just don't offer enough room to properly toss and stir bulky noodles and ingredients. I also strongly recommend a good-quality non-stick wok. Noodles can stick to carbon-steel woks that are not well-seasoned, making a mess and requiring more oil. A wok or stir-fry pan coated with a high-quality, durable, non-stick such as Excalibur®, which is used on my line of non-stick woks and stir-fry pans, and which I used to test all the stir-fry noodle recipes, works very well as the noodles will cook in less oil without sticking.

knife

Just as important as a good wok is a good knife. I am not referring to a large, heavy cleaver, made of a softer steel for chopping, but the lighter, mid-size Asian cleavers (I prefer to call them Chinese chef knives) designed for cutting and slicing vegetables and boneless meats. The knives I prefer to use are either a medium-weight Chinese chef knife (or cleaver) or a Japanese santoku. A high-quality stainless steel is much easier to maintain and won't rust, stain, or give a metallic taste to foods. A good knife should be well-balanced and weighted so it feels like an extension of your hand. Use a sharpening steel occasionally to keep the edge nice and sharp.

chopsticks

For stirring and tossing stringy noodles, a sturdy pair of bamboo cooking chopsticks used in conjunction with a spatula is very handy. Chopsticks are also useful for removing pieces of ginger and garlic from finished dishes and for picking up noodles and other morsels for tasting.

wire strainer

Also known as a "spider," this long bamboo-handled woven wire strainer is indispensable for quickly and efficiently straining and lifting noodles, wontons, and other ingredients from hot oil, boiling water, or broth.

spatula

I like bamboo spatulas because they are strong, durable, gentle to any cooking surface, dishwasher-safe, and affordable. Choose spatulas with rounded corners so they reach into the rounded sides of woks and stir-fry pans.

ginger grater

Most recipes require slices of fresh ginger, but some of them call for grated ginger. Made of stainless steel or porcelain, Asian ginger graters have sharp raised teeth that pull out only the ginger pulp, leaving the tough strings behind.

asian mandoline

One of my favorite tools is the Asian mandoline. Hand shredding can be tedious and time-consuming, but this compact tool is wonderful. One of my favorite mandolines is made by the Benriner Co., Ltd. in Japan. It is used throughout Japan and is popular with professional chefs in America as well. The Benriner mandoline is available with its own see-through catch tray and 3 interchangeable shredding blades for fine, medium, or wide shreds. The resulting shreds are perfectly cut and the right size and shape for Asian cooking. You won't have to shy away from recipes calling for shredded ingredients again.

glossary of ingredients

bean paste or bean sauce

Thick, salty, fermented soybean paste is used as a base for many sauces. It is available in whole bean, pureed form, or spicy hot Sichuan style. I prefer using the pureed bean paste. Both are available in cans or glass jars.

The Japanese make an excellent-quality bean paste called miso that is packed in refrigerated sealed plastic bags or plastic tubs. There are many varieties of miso available, mainly white (*shiro* miso) and red (*aka* miso). White miso is used when a lighter, sweeter taste is desired, while red miso provides a heartier, more robust flavor. Store bean paste in the refrigerator after opening.

chili-garlic sauce

I don't always have fresh chilies on hand, but when I want to "heat" up a dish quickly, I use Vietnamese chili-garlic sauce. This sauce may be used in cooking or as a condiment at the table. It's easy to control the spiciness of a dish by simply reducing or increasing the amount of chili-garlic sauce used. The most popular and well-known brand is from Huy Fong Foods, Inc. It comes in a plastic jar with a bright green lid and a rooster logo on the front. This company also produces excellent *sambal oelek* and *Sriracha* hot chile sauce, both of which may be used as substitutes.

chinese rice wine

Shaoxing wine from Zhejiang province in China is famous for its high-quality cooking and drinking rice wine. Chinese rice wines used for cooking are available in Asian markets, but don't try to serve it as a table wine because they are usually salted. Pale, dry sherry is an excellent substitute.

chinese cabbage (*bai cai*—mandarin, *bok choy*—cantonese)

There are many varieties of Chinese cabbage available in the marketplace, but there are basically two varieties that I use most often. The first is napa cabbage, a variety of Chinese cabbage that is light green with crinkly leaves and a stout, compact shape. It's a great emergency ingredient and I always have it in my refrigerator.

The other variety I like is Shanghai bok choy, sometimes called baby bok choy. Instead of long thick white stems, Shanghai bok choy is smaller, about 6 inches long with delicate green leaves and stems.

cilantro (also known as fresh coriander or chinese parsley)

The Chinese call cilantro *xiang cai*, or "fragrant vegetable," and so it is. It resembles flat-leaf parsley but has a strong, distinctive aroma. Some people, especially children, find the taste too strong and claim that it tastes like soap. Interestingly enough, there is a small percentage of people who never outgrow their dislike for this herb. You may wish to ask your guests about their preferences before you use it in your dish.

coconut milk

Coconut milk is not the liquid found in coconuts, but comes from grated coconuts and adds creaminess and flavor to soups, curries, and desserts. Don't confuse this unsweetened liquid with the thick sweetened coconut cream used to make cocktails such as piña coladas. The brand I prefer is Chaokoh from Thailand.

dried black mushrooms

These are dried shiitake mushrooms. Asians like to use dried mushrooms because the smoky flavor is more concentrated and pronounced. They must be soaked in hot water to soften before use. The soaking water is useful and may be strained and added to soups or used for additional moisture in stir-fries.

fermented black beans (or salted black beans or dried black beans)

Don't confuse these with dried black beans used in Mexican cooking. These are whole soybeans that have been salted and aged with spices. They have a rich, robust, salty taste and soft texture. A little goes a long way, so be judicious with their use.

fish sauce

Extracted from fermented anchovies and salt, this pungent sauce is to the Southeast Asians as soy sauce is to the Chinese. Known as *nuoc mam* in Vietnam, and *nam pla* in Thailand, this salty, clear amber liquid is essential to both Vietnamese and Thai cuisine. The brands I like to use are Viet Huong Three Crabs, Squid, or Tiparos.

five-spice powder

This prepared spice powder is made with about five (sometimes more) different ground spices, including cinnamon, star anise, licorice, cloves, fennel, ginger, anise seed, and pepper. Store tightly covered in a cool, dark, dry place as you would other powdered spices.

garlic chives

Also known as Chinese chives, these long grass-like leaves are flat rather than round and have a stronger flavor and texture than regular chives. It's an easy-to-grow perennial and sports lovely white flowers that are also edible. If not available, substitute scallions.

lemongrass

This fragrant grass-like herb is widely used in Southeast Asian cuisine and is often available in well-stocked supermarkets. In the West it is known as citronella. Only the tender heart of the bulb is used, and is either sliced, minced, or bruised so its lemony scent perfumes the dish. The tougher pieces are removed before serving. I recommend using only fresh lemongrass for the best flavor. Substitute with lemon rind.

mirin

Made from fermented glutinous rice, mirin is a sweet rice cooking wine used instead of sugar by the Japanese. Its sweetness figures prominently in many Japanese dishes and gives the glossy sheen to cooked meats such as teriyaki and yakitori.

miso

See Bean paste (page 16).

nori (also known as laver)

These thin, dark sheets of seaweed are commonly used to make rolled sushi. The Japanese also shred nori into thin strips to use as a garnish. To shred, fold a sheet of nori in half or thirds and cut with a sharp knife or scissors into thin shreds.

oyster sauce

This versatile and tasty Cantonese cooking sauce, also called oyster-flavored sauce, is made from oyster extract, salt, and spices. Contrary to its name, this thick brown sauce does not taste like oysters. My favorite brand is from Lee Kum Kee and called Premium Oyster Flavored Sauce. Refrigerate after opening.

sesame oil

Asian sesame oil is pressed from roasted sesame seeds, hence its dark amber color and heady fragrance. Its low smoking temperature and strong flavor make it unsuitable for stir-frying, but perfect as a garnishing oil for dressings, dips, or added to fillings for added flavor.

sichuan peppercorns

Unrelated to black peppercorns, these dried reddish-brown berries are widely used in Sichuan cuisine for cooking, as well as for pickling and curing meats. They are generally toasted and ground before use.

sichuan preserved vegetable

The knobby, fleshy stems of a particular kind of mustard green are preserved in salt and chili powder for this Sichuan specialty. Its salty, sour, spicy taste and crisp texture enrich soups and stir-fry dishes. Sichuan vegetable comes in cans and is available whole or shredded. I like to buy the shredded version because it is easier to use. Always rinse before using since it is heavily salted. Once opened, it will keep indefinitely if stored in a tightly lidded glass container in the refrigerator. The brand I recommend is the Ma Ling brand from China labeled Zhejiang Preserved Vegetable.

snow cabbage

This pickled vegetable is known as "Red-in-Snow" to the Shanghainese. It refers to the fact that the roots of this mustard green are red and often sprout through the snow in early spring. The leaves are pickled in brine and have a distinctive salty, pungent taste. Pickled snow cabbage is used as a condiment and flavoring. It is available in cans.

soy sauce

There are two main kinds of soy sauce used in Chinese cooking—light and dark. Light soy sauce refers to the thin texture of the sauce and may be substituted with Japanese soy sauce. Dark soy sauce contains molasses, which gives it a darker color, slightly sweet taste, and thicker texture. I always keep both types on hand.

star anise

This lovely spice, which some of you will recognize from art class, has five to eight cloves that form a star. The Chinese name of *ba jiao* means "eight corners." Use star anise whole or break off cloves.

thai basil

The dark green-purple leaves of this aromatic herb have a distinctive basil and licorice flavor and are essential to Thai and Vietnamese cuisines. Its fresh leaves are used as a garnish or ingredient in soups, stir-fried dishes, and cold salads. You may substitute with sweet basil.

yu choy (also known as *yow choy* in cantonese or *yu cai* in mandarin)

Here's a leafy green loved and commonly used by the Cantonese. The Chinese name is translated as "oil vegetable" because oil is produced from their seeds. If unavailable, substitute almost any other leafy green such as spinach, watercress, bok choy, or napa cabbage.

stir-fried, pan-fried, and sauced

ants climbing a tree

This easy Sichuan dish can be made as hot and spicy as you like by simply adjusting the amount of chili-garlic sauce. These fine, thin noodles, called bean thread, are made from mung beans, the same beans that give us bean sprouts. When these noodles are softened and cooked they become transparent, so they are also known by other names such as cellophane or glass noodles. With a little imagination the bits of pork that cling to the noodle strands resemble ants crawling up branches of a tree, hence the fanciful name. ■ SERVES 3 TO 4

½ pound ground pork

4 tablespoons light soy sauce

2 teaspoons Chinese cooking wine or dry sherry

2 teaspoons sugar

2 teaspoons cornstarch

4 ounces bean thread

4 medium dried black mushrooms

2 tablespoons canola oil

3 slices unpeeled fresh ginger

3 scallions, bulbs split in half and cut into 1-inch pieces

1 teaspoon to 1 tablespoon chili-garlic sauce, to taste

1 teaspoon sesame oil

¼ cup chopped cilantro (fresh coriander)

1 In a medium mixing bowl, combine the pork with soy sauce, wine, sugar, and cornstarch together.

2 Soak the bean thread in hot (not boiling) water until soft. Drain carefully and cut into shorter lengths with scissors. Set aside and drain well. Soak the mushrooms in hot water for 15 minutes to soften. Drain the mushrooms, reserving 2 tablespoons of the soaking liquid. Squeeze dry. Cut off the stems with scissors and discard. Shred the caps.

3 In a wok or stir-fry pan, heat the canola oil over high heat until hot, but not smoking. Add the ginger and stir for a few seconds as the ginger sizzles. Add the pork mixture and cook, stirring constantly, until the pork breaks up, about 2 minutes.

4 Add the mushrooms and scallions, stirring constantly for another minute or until the pork is cooked through. Add the chili-garlic sauce, bean thread, and the reserved liquid from the mushrooms, and cook, stirring, until the noodles become transparent and the pork is well incorporated into the noodles, about 2 minutes; do not overcook or the bean thread will become too soft and mushy.

5 Drizzle with sesame oil and give the noodles a couple of big turns with the spatula. Remove and discard the ginger, if desired. Transfer to a platter, sprinkle with cilantro, and serve immediately.

crispy noodle cake with shredded chicken and vegetables

You can pan-fry the noodles at the same time you are stir-frying the topping, keeping an eye on both pans at once. Or, if that's too hectic, pan-fry the noodles first and keep them warm in a moderate oven as you cook the topping. Eat the noodles as soon as you can after browning while they are still hot and crunchy. If you don't feel like having noodles, the topping is also delicious served with steamed rice. ■ SERVES 3 TO 4

½ pound Chinese egg noodles

8 tablespoons canola oil

2 tablespoons plus 2 teaspoons cornstarch

2 teaspoons Chinese rice wine or dry sherry

½ pound skinless, boneless chicken breast, shredded, about 1 cup (see page 23)

1¼ cups canned chicken broth

2 tablespoons oyster sauce

1 tablespoon light soy sauce

1 teaspoon sugar

3 slices unpeeled fresh ginger

1 teaspoon minced garlic

1 cup thinly sliced onions

1 cup white mushrooms, stems trimmed and thinly sliced

1 stalk celery, thinly sliced on the diagonal

½ cup sliced canned bamboo shoots, drained

3 cups fresh bean sprouts

½ teaspoon salt, or to taste

1 In a large pot of boiling water, cook the noodles until a little more tender than al dente. Taste often to be sure they do not over-cook. When tender, drain and rinse in cold water. Drain thoroughly and mix with 2 tablespoons of the oil to prevent them from sticking together. Set aside.

2 In a small mixing bowl, whisk together 2 teaspoons of the corn-starch and the wine. Add the chicken and stir well. In a separate bowl, dissolve the remaining 2 tablespoons of cornstarch in ¼ cup of the broth. In a third bowl, stir together the remaining 1 cup broth and the oyster sauce, soy sauce, and sugar.

3 In a large (11-inch) non-stick skillet or heavy pan, heat 4 table-spoons of the oil, over medium-high heat. Swirl the oil around the pan so the sides as well as the bottom are coated. The oil is ready when one noodle placed in the oil sizzles. Add the noodles and spread them out to the edges of the pan. Fry the noodles until they are golden brown, 8 to 10 minutes on each side. Lift and peek every so often to see how they are browning. When the first side has browned, flip the noodles over and fry the other side. Transfer to a cutting board and cut into quarters, like a pizza. This will make for easier serving later on. Transfer and reassemble the noodles on a large serving platter and place in a warm oven or stir-fry the topping while the second side is browning.

4 To make the topping, pour the remaining 2 tablespoons of oil into a wok or stir-fry pan and place the pan over high heat. Add the ginger and garlic and stir around the pan until they begin to sizzle. Mix up the chicken again, pour it into the pan, and cook, stirring, until the meat separates and turns white, about 2 minutes. Remove and discard the ginger, if desired. Add the onions, mushrooms, celery, and bamboo shoots and cook, stirring, until the vegetables are well-mixed and tender-crisp, about 2 minutes. Add the bean sprouts and cook, stirring constantly, until the sprouts are incorporated into the mixture, about 1 minute. Stir in the salt and broth mixture. When it comes to a boil, add the well-stirred cornstarch slurry and stir until the sauce thickens.

5 Transfer the noodles from the oven or from the skillet to a platter. Mound the sauce and topping over the noodle cake and serve immediately.

how to shred chicken and pork

Meat is best shred to the size and shape of a matchstick or bean sprout. It is easier to shred meat if it is partially frozen—about 20 minutes in the freezer will firm it up, but not make it too hard to cut.

TO SHRED PORK: For pork, I prefer to use thin-cut boneless chops. They are less expensive and are often thin enough that they do not need to be split before shredding. Thicker chops can be split and then shredded. With the knife horizontal to the cutting board split the meat into three or four pieces depending on the thickness of the chop. Pile up the pieces and cut the meat into ⅛-inch shreds. Be sure to trim off the fat first.

To shred pork tenderloin, cut thin slices, then stack them up and cut across into shreds.

TO SHRED BONELESS CHICKEN BREAST: Remove the skin and discard. With the knife blade horizontal to the cutting board, split the breast into two to four thin, flat pieces depending on the thickness of the breast. Pile the pieces on top of each other and cut across into ⅛-inch shreds.

cantonese pork lo mein

Lo mein means "tossed noodles" in Cantonese. If Chinese noodles are unavailable, substitute vermicelli or thin spaghetti. Tiny dried salted shrimp, available in Asian markets, are often used as a flavoring in salads, soups, and stir-fried dishes. If you can't find Chinese dried shrimp, omit them and add a little more soy sauce to taste. ■ SERVES 3 TO 4

½ pound Chinese wheat or egg noodles

1 tablespoon Chinese rice wine or dry sherry

1 tablespoon light soy sauce

1 teaspoon cornstarch

8 ounces shredded lean pork (about 1 cup) (see page 23)

1 tablespoon dried shrimp

4 tablespoons canola oil

2 garlic cloves, crushed with the side of a knife and peeled

5 scallions, bulbs split and cut into 1-inch lengths

3 tablespoons oyster sauce

3 tablespoons canned chicken broth

1 teaspoon sesame oil

¼ teaspoon freshly ground white pepper, or more to taste

1 In a large pot of boiling water, cook the noodles until a little softer than al dente. This should take no more than 2 minutes if the noodles are the pre-cooked variety. Drain, rinse in cold water, drain again thoroughly, and set aside.

2 In a small bowl, whisk together 1 teaspoon of the wine, the soy sauce, and the cornstarch. Add the pork and mix thoroughly.

3 Put the dried shrimp in a small dish and pour the remaining 2 teaspoons of wine over them. Set aside to soften.

4 In a wok or stir-fry pan, heat 3 tablespoons of the canola oil over medium-high heat. Add the garlic and stir until the oil is hot and the garlic sizzles. Add the noodles and cook, stirring occasionally, until the noodles begin to lightly brown, 4 to 5 minutes. Remove and discard the garlic, if desired. Transfer the noodles to a plate lined with paper towels to absorb any excess oil.

5 Pour the remaining 1 tablespoon canola oil into the same pan. Add the well-stirred pork mixture and cook, stirring, for about 2 minutes, or until there is no pink left in the meat. Add the shrimp mixture and scallions and cook, stirring, until the scallions turn a darker green and wilt. Return the noodles to the pan. Add the oyster sauce and broth and cook, stirring, until the sauce is evenly absorbed into the noodles. Add the sesame oil and pepper and toss well. Transfer to a plate and serve immediately.

peking meat-sauced noodles

My mother often used packaged spaghetti or vermicelli for this dish, because in the early 1950s using Chinese egg noodles meant a special trip to Chinatown. When we had this dish in China, it was at a tiny restaurant that had a "noodle stretcher," a man who stretched noodles by hand. After he stretched the noodles, helpers immediately dropped them into a large vat of boiling water, then strained them right into a large noodle bowl. They scooped up a large ladle of sauce, poured it on, and added a crunchy vegetable garnish. People were lined up waiting to lunch on a bowl of those Peking noodles! They were delicious, but I've always liked my mother's better. You may substitute ground turkey for the pork. Both are equally delicious! ■ SERVES 6 TO 8

---

1 teaspoon Chinese rice wine or dry sherry

1 teaspoon cornstarch

½ pound ground pork (about 1 cup)

½ cup bean paste, preferably Japanese red miso

2 tablespoons hoisin sauce

2 tablespoons dark soy sauce

1 tablespoon sugar

2 tablespoons canola oil

1 medium onion, minced

1 teaspoon minced garlic

½ cup thinly sliced scallions

1 pound Chinese wheat or egg noodles, or thin or regular spaghetti

10 radishes, shredded, for garnish

1 medium cucumber, partially peeled (leaving a few long strips of peel on the sides), seeded, and shredded, for garnish

1 In a small bowl, mix the wine and cornstarch together. Add the pork and mix well. In a separate small bowl, stir the bean paste, hoisin sauce, soy sauce, and sugar together.

2 In a wok or stir-fry pan, heat the oil over high heat. When the oil is hot, but not smoking, add the pork mixture and cook, stirring constantly, until the meat changes color and breaks up, about 2 minutes. Add the onion and garlic and stir for another minute. Add the scallions and cook, stirring constantly, until the scallions are soft but not browned, another minute.

3 Stir in the bean paste mixture and 1 cup water and mix thoroughly. Turn the heat to low and simmer for 3 to 4 minutes, stirring occasionally. You will have a thin sauce.

4 Meanwhile, in a large pot, bring 5 quarts of water to a boil. Stir in the spaghetti and boil until a little more tender than al dente. Drain and rinse in hot water; immediately divide the noodles among 6 or 8 individual noodle bowls. Place the meat sauce in a serving bowl on the table. Set the vegetable garnishes out in individual bowls and let people sauce and garnish their own noodles.

2 cups bean sprouts, parboiled for 15 to 20 seconds, drained, rinsed in cold water, and drained well, for garnish

10 ounces fresh spinach, washed, parboiled for 15 to 20 seconds, rinsed in cold water, squeezed dry, and minced, for garnish

5 garlic cloves, peeled and finely minced, for garnish (optional, see Note)

Note: Northern Chinese have a propensity toward garlic—cooked or raw—and lots of it! The caveat to adding raw garlic garnish to these noodles is: if you're going out on a date or social occasion, leave them out.

noodles with shredded pork, bean sprouts, and sichuan preserved vegetable

When I need a small amount of pork, I use thin boneless chops. They are lean and economical. If the chop is thick, partially freeze it and split it in half or thirds lengthwise, then pile the pieces on top of one another and cut across into thin shreds. The thinner the shreds, the better they will incorporate into the noodles. This dish is also delicious served at room temperature—a boon on hot summer nights. ■ SERVES 4 TO 6

12 ounces Chinese wheat or egg noodles, or vermicelli

5 tablespoons light soy sauce

1 tablespoon Chinese rice wine or dry sherry

2 teaspoons cornstarch

½ pound lean pork, shredded (about 1 cup) (see page 23)

1 teaspoon sugar

2 tablespoons canola oil

1½ teaspoons minced garlic

1 teaspoon peeled and minced fresh ginger

8 ounces fresh bean sprouts

½ cup shredded Sichuan preserved vegetable, rinsed and drained

3 scallions, bulbs split and cut into 1-inch pieces

2 teaspoons sesame oil

1 In a large pot of boiling water, cook the noodles until a little softer than al dente. Drain, rinse in cold water and set aside to drain again.

2 In a medium mixing bowl, whisk together 1 tablespoon of the soy sauce, the wine, and the cornstarch. Add the pork and mix together. In a separate small dish, combine the remaining 4 tablespoons soy sauce and the sugar. Stir to dissolve the sugar.

3 In a wok or stir-fry pan, heat the canola oil over medium-high heat. When the oil is hot, but not smoking, add the garlic and ginger and stir until they sizzle; do not allow the garlic to burn. Stir up the pork again and add it to the pan, stirring quickly until the meat separates and all the pink is almost gone, about 2 minutes.

4 Add the bean sprouts, Sichuan preserved vegetable, and scallions. Stir until the scallions turn a darker green, about 2 minutes. Lightly rinse the noodles with a little tap water to loosen, drain and add them to the pan, and pour the soy sauce mixture over them. Cook, stirring, and tossing until the noodles are heated through and evenly colored. Pour the sesame oil over the noodles and toss to distribute evenly. Transfer to a serving platter and serve immediately.

beef and broccoli on crispy noodle cake

Shanghai people call this "Two-Sides-Brown" because the boiled noodles are pan-fried on both sides to a crispy golden brown on the outside while the noodles inside stay soft and chewy. A saucy stir-fried topping is mounded on top before serving. Since pan-frying the noodles can take as much as 20 minutes, there's plenty of time to stir-fry the topping at the same time the noodles are browning. Alternatively, the browned noodles may be placed in a warm (250°F) oven while the topping is being cooked. ■ SERVES 3 TO 4

½ pound Chinese egg noodles

8 tablespoons canola oil

½ pound broccoli

12 ounces beef flank steak, trimmed

3 tablespoons dark soy sauce

2 teaspoons Chinese rice wine or dry sherry

2 tablespoons plus 3 teaspoons cornstarch

1 teaspoon sugar

1¼ cups canned chicken broth

3 tablespoons oyster sauce

2 slices unpeeled fresh ginger

2 teaspoons minced garlic

1 cup shredded red bell peppers

1 cup sliced white mushrooms

1 (8-ounce) can sliced bamboo shoots, drained

3 scallions, bulbs split and cut into 2-inch lengths

1 In a large pot of boiling water, cook the noodles until a little more tender than al dente. Be sure not to overcook. If the noodles are fresh they will cook in a very short time. Taste often as they cook. When tender, drain and rinse in cold water. Drain thoroughly and toss with 2 tablespoons of the oil to prevent them from sticking together.

2 Trim and peel the broccoli stalk. Cut the crown into 2-inch long florets and the stem into bite-size pieces. Blanch the broccoli in boiling water until just tender, about 30 seconds. Drain immediately and run under cold water to stop the cooking.

3 Slice the beef along the grain into long strips about 2 inches wide. Slice the long pieces against the grain into very thin slices, about ⅛ inch thick. In a medium bowl, whisk together 1 tablespoon of the soy sauce, the wine, 3 teaspoons of the cornstarch, and the sugar. Add the meat and stir together well. In a separate bowl, dissolve the remaining 2 tablespoons of cornstarch in ¼ cup of the broth. In a third small bowl, combine the oyster sauce, remaining 2 tablespoons soy sauce, and ¼ cup broth.

4 In a large (11-inch) non-stick skillet or other flat-bottom heavy pan, heat 4 tablespoons of the oil over medium-high heat until hot. Swirl the oil so the sides as well as the bottom of the pan are coated. The oil is ready when a noodle placed in the oil sizzles. Add the noodles and spread them out evenly to the edges of the pan. Reduce heat to medium and fry until the noodles are golden brown,

(continued)

8 to 10 minutes on each side. Don't rush this step by turning the heat too high or else the noodles will end up burning, and not browning. Lift and peek every so often to see how they are browning. When the first side has browned, turn the noodles over using two spatulas and fry the other side. While the second side is browning, start cooking the topping so that both will be done at the same time.

5 To make the topping, pour the remaining 2 tablespoons of oil into a wok or stir-fry pan and place the pan over high heat. Add the ginger and garlic and stir around the pan until they begin to sizzle. Remove and discard the ginger, if desired. Mix up the meat again, pour it into the pan, and stir until almost cooked through, about 2 minutes. Add the broccoli, bell pepper, mushrooms, bamboo shoots, and scallions to the pan. Cook, stirring constantly, until the vegetables are well mixed, about 1 minute. Pour in the oyster sauce mixture and remaining ¾ cup of broth and cook, stirring. When the liquid comes to a boil add the cornstarch slurry and stir until the sauce thickens. Remove and discard the ginger, if desired. Remove from the heat.

6 Transfer the fried noodle cake to a cutting board and cut it into quarters, like a pizza. This will make it easier to serve later on. Transfer and reassemble the noodles on a large platter and pour the topping and all the sauce over the noodles. Serve immediately.

yaki-soba

Chuka soba, which translates as "Chinese noodles," are pre-cooked wheat noodles that are dried and packed in blocks, much like the familiar ramen noodles. The word *soba* conjures up buckwheat noodles, but in this context it is used as a general term for noodles. Worcestershire sauce provides the main flavoring, but you can also use bottled *yaki-soba* or *tonkatsu* sauce, which is used on classic breaded and pan-fried pork cutlets. In Japan, *yaki-soba* is a popular fast-food dish and commonly available at street food stalls. ■ Serves 3 to 4

½ pound *chuka soba* noodles or thin spaghetti

2 teaspoons Chinese cooking wine or dry sherry

1 teaspoon cornstarch

6 ounces skinless, boneless chicken breast or pork tenderloin, shredded (see page 23), about ¾ cup

¼ cup canned chicken broth

2 tablespoons Worcestershire sauce

2 tablespoons oyster sauce

1 tablespoon light soy sauce

¼ teaspoon freshly ground black pepper

3 tablespoons canola oil

2 slices unpeeled fresh ginger

1 cup shredded red bell peppers

1 cup shredded zucchini

2 medium napa cabbage leaves, cut across into ½-inch pieces

1 medium carrot, shredded

2 scallions, thinly sliced

1 In a large pot of boiling water, cook the noodles until a little more tender than al dente. *Chuka soba* noodles are pre-cooked and therefore cook very fast. Be careful not to overcook. Drain, rinse in cold water, and set aside to drain again.

2 In a mixing bowl, whisk together the wine and cornstarch then add the chicken and mix thoroughly.

3 In a separate small bowl combine the broth, Worcestershire sauce, oyster sauce, soy sauce, and pepper.

4 In a wok or stir-fry pan, heat the oil over medium-high heat. Add the ginger and stir until the oil is hot and the ginger sizzles; do not allow the oil to smoke. Mix the chicken once again and add to the pan. Cook, stirring constantly, until the meat is almost cooked, about 2 minutes.

5 Add the pepper, zucchini, cabbage, and carrot, and cook, stirring, until the vegetables are tender-crisp, about 2 minutes. Remove and discard the ginger, if desired.

6 Sprinkle the noodles with a few tablespoons of tap water to loosen, drain, then add the noodles to the pan and pour in the sauce mixture and scallions. Cook, stirring constantly, until thoroughly mixed and the noodles are heated through. Serve immediately.

delights of three pan-fried noodles

Numerology figures prominently in Chinese lore and culture. Lucky numbers abound, with the number eight being very auspicious for the southern Chinese. Four has a negative connotation since the word is a homonym for "death," so three works out better. Here, the three delights are pork, chicken, and shrimp all in one dish. ■ SERVES 3 TO 4

½ pound Chinese egg noodles

8 tablespoons canola oil

8 teaspoons cornstarch

2 tablespoons light soy sauce

3 teaspoons Chinese rice wine or dry sherry

4 ounces lean pork, shredded (see page 23), about ½ cup

4 ounces skinless, boneless chicken breast or thigh, shredded (see page 23), about ½ cup

4 ounces large shrimp, shelled, de-veined and split in half lengthwise

1½ cups canned chicken broth

1 cup medium dried black mushrooms, soaked in hot water for 15 minutes until soft

2 teaspoons peeled and finely minced ginger

6 ounces shredded napa cabbage or Shanghai bok choy

½ cup canned sliced bamboo shoots, drained

3 scallions, cut into 1-inch pieces

¼ teaspoon freshly ground white pepper

¼ teaspoon salt, to taste

1 In a large pot of boiling water, cook the noodles until a little more tender than al dente. Be sure not to overcook. If the noodles are fresh they will cook in a very short time. Taste often as they cook. When tender, drain and rinse in cold water. Drain thoroughly and mix with 2 tablespoons of the oil to prevent them from sticking together. Set aside.

2 In a medium mixing bowl, whisk together 1 teaspoon of the cornstarch, 1 tablespoon of soy sauce, and 2 teaspoons of wine. Add the pork and chicken and mix well. In a separate small bowl, whisk together 1 teaspoon of the cornstarch and 1 teaspoon of the wine. Add the shrimp and mix well. In a third small bowl, dissolve the remaining 6 teaspoons of cornstarch in ½ cup of broth and stir in the remaining tablespoon of soy sauce. Drain the mushrooms and squeeze dry. Cut off the stems with scissors and discard. Shred the caps.

3 In a large (11-inch) non-stick skillet or other flat-bottomed heavy pan, heat 4 tablespoons of the oil over medium-high heat. The oil is hot when a noodle placed in the pan sizzles. Add the noodles and spread them out to the edges of the pan. Reduce the heat to medium and fry until the noodles are golden brown, 8 to 10 minutes for each side. Lift and check occasionally to see how they are browning. When the first side has browned, with two spatulas, flip the noodles over and fry the other side in the same manner. Cook the topping as the second side is browning, or brown both sides of the noodles and place in a warm (250°F) oven until ready to serve.

4 To make the topping, pour the remaining 2 tablespoons of oil into a wok or stir-fry pan and place the pan over high heat. Add the ginger and stir around the pan until it begins to sizzle. Mix up the meat again, pour it into the pan, and cook, stirring briskly, until the meat separates and all the pink is gone, about 2 minutes. Add the well-stirred shrimp mixture and cook, stirring, until the shrimp starts to turn pink. Add the mushrooms, cabbage, bamboo shoots, and scallions and cook, stirring, until the cabbage wilts and the scallions turn a darker green, about 3 minutes. Add the remaining cup of broth and when the liquid comes to a boil, pour in the well-mixed cornstarch slurry, stirring constantly until the sauce thickens. Sprinkle with the pepper and salt and stir to mix evenly.

5 Transfer the noodles from the oven or skillet to a cutting board and cut into quarters, like a pizza. Reassemble on a large platter and spoon the topping and all the sauce over the noodles. Serve immediately.

chinese home-style soft fried noodles

This is a versatile noodle recipe that allows for a multitude of substitutions and additions. Instead of the pork use chicken, or beef, or leave the meat out entirely. In addition to the cabbage you may add a couple of ounces each of spinach leaves and bean sprouts, or some shredded carrots, zucchini, and red bell pepper. Keep the vegetables to a total of about 4 to 5 cups and adjust the seasoning by increasing the soy sauce and salt. My mother used to serve this to us as a simple lunch dish when we were children. Our favorite condiment? Ketchup. Try it, or vinegar, and you'll be amazed how this brightens up the flavor! Even today, I still enjoy these noodles with a dollop of ketchup mixed in. ■ SERVES 3 TO 4

½ pound Chinese wheat or egg noodles, or vermicelli or thin spaghetti

1 teaspoon Chinese rice wine or dry sherry

1 teaspoon cornstarch

½ cup shredded pork, chicken, or beef (see page 23), about 8 ounces

2 tablespoons light soy sauce, or to taste

½ teaspoon sugar

3 medium dried black mushrooms, soaked in hot water for 15 minutes until soft

3 tablespoons canola oil

2 cups shredded napa cabbage

½ cup sliced canned bamboo shoots, drained

½ teaspoon salt, or to taste

1 In a large pot of boiling water, cook the noodles until a little softer than al dente. Drain, rinse in cold water, and set aside to drain again.

2 In a mixing bowl, stir together the wine and cornstarch, then add the meat and stir again. In a separate bowl, mix together the soy sauce and sugar. Drain the mushrooms and squeeze dry. Cut off the stems with scissors and discard. Shred the caps.

3 In a wok or stir-fry pan, heat the oil over medium-high heat. When the oil is hot, but not smoking, add the meat mixture and cook, stirring, until it separates and changes color, about 1 minute. Add the cabbage, bamboo shoots, and mushrooms and stir until the cabbage begins to wilt, 1 to 2 minutes. Stir in the salt.

4 Sprinkle the noodles with a few tablespoons of water to loosen them up, drain, then add them to the pan. Pour the soy sauce mixture over the noodles and stir until evenly colored, about 30 seconds. If more vegetables are desired add the spinach and bean sprouts with the noodles and cook, stirring, until the vegetables are wilted, yet still tender-crisp, about 3 minutes. Transfer the noodles to a platter and serve immediately with (or without) ketchup and vinegar.

mixed seafood on soft noodles

This naturally low in fat seafood topping accompanies boiled noodles instead of the traditional pan-fried crispy noodles, saving both calories and time. This whole dish actually calls for only two tablespoons of cooking oil! The combination of different seafood is not uncommon in the Chinese cooking repertoire. It makes for a rich yet subtle flavor. ■ SERVES 3 TO 4

½ pound Chinese egg or wheat noodles

4 ounces squid, cleaned

2 teaspoons Chinese cooking wine or dry sherry

7 teaspoons cornstarch

½ teaspoon salt, or to taste

4 ounces sea scallops, cut in half or quarters if large

4 ounces large shrimp (21/30), deveined and split in half lengthwise

1½ cups canned chicken broth

2 tablespoons light soy sauce

2 tablespoons canola oil

2 slices unpeeled fresh ginger

1 (8-ounce) can sliced bamboo shoots, drained

½ cup canned straw mushrooms, drained

3 scallions, bulbs split and cut into 2-inch lengths

6 ounces leafy green vegetable, such as *yu choy*, broccoli rabe, or *bai cai*, cut into 2-inch sections

1 teaspoon sesame oil

¼ teaspoon freshly ground white pepper, or to taste

1 In a large pot of boiling water, cook the noodles until a little softer than al dente. Remove the noodles with a wire strainer and reserve the boiling water for reheating the noodles later. Rinse the noodles in cold water and set aside to drain again.

2 Rinse the squid inside and out with cold water and drain. Cut down one side of the body tube and spread out flat with the inside facing up. Lightly score the flesh in a fine crisscross pattern and cut into pieces about 2 to 3 inches square. If the head with the tentacles is large, cut in half.

3 In a medium mixing bowl, whisk the wine with 2 teaspoons of the cornstarch, and ¼ teaspoon salt. Add the squid, scallops, and shrimp and mix together.

4 In a separate bowl, combine 1 cup broth with the soy sauce. In a third bowl, dissolve the remaining 5 teaspoons of cornstarch in the remaining ½ cup broth.

5 In a wok or stir-fry pan, heat the canola oil and ginger over high heat. When the ginger sizzles add the bamboo shoots, straw mushrooms, and scallions and cook, stirring, until the scallions turn a darker green, about 1 minute. Add the greens and cook, stirring, until they turn a darker green, about another minute. Add the well-stirred seafood mixture and cook, stirring, for another minute or until the shrimp and squid begin to curl and lose their transparent look. Add the broth mixture and when the liquid comes to a boil,

(continued)

stir the cornstarch mixture again and add it to the pan. Cook, stirring, until the sauce thickens. Add the sesame oil, the remaining ¼ teaspoon of salt, and the pepper, stir to mix and remove from the heat. Remove and discard the ginger, if desired.

6 Reheat the noodles by plunging them into the reserved pot of boiling water for about 30 seconds until heated through or pour a kettle of boiling water over them. Drain well and transfer noodles to a shallow platter. Pour the topping over the noodles and serve immediately.

> ■ VARIATION: Watercress also works well as the green vegetable. Rinse and cut in half. Watercress cooks quickly, so add it to the pan with the broth in step 4, then continue.

mahogany noodles

This is a meatless stir-fry noodle that can be served hot or cold. The fragrant Sichuan peppercorns bring a deep aromatic flavor to this dish, while the dark soy sauce colors the noodles a shiny dark brown. Half a teaspoon of the chili-garlic sauce will give the noodles a hint of spice; increase to 1 teaspoon and the heat can be felt; add 1 tablespoon or more for breathing fire. ■ SERVES 4 AS A SIDE DISH

6 ounces Chinese egg or wheat noodles or vermicelli or thin spaghetti

2 tablespoons dark soy sauce

1 tablespoon cider vinegar

1 teaspoon Chinese cooking wine or pale dry sherry

1 teaspoon sesame oil

1 teaspoon chili-garlic sauce, or more to taste

1 tablespoon sugar

1 teaspoon Sichuan peppercorns, toasted and ground (see page 108)

1 tablespoon canola oil

1½ teaspoons peeled and minced fresh ginger

1 teaspoon finely minced garlic

2 scallions, bulbs split and cut into 1-inch pieces

1 In a large pot of boiling water, cook the noodles until a little softer than al dente. Drain, rinse in cold water and set aside to drain again.

2 In a small mixing bowl, whisk together the soy sauce, vinegar, wine, sesame oil, chili-garlic sauce, sugar, and peppercorn powder.

3 In a wok or stir-fry pan, heat the canola oil over medium-high heat. Add the ginger and garlic and stir until the oil is hot and the garlic and ginger sizzle; do not allow the garlic to burn. Sprinkle the noodles with a few tablespoons of water to loosen, drain, and add them to the pan. Pour the soy sauce mixture over the noodles and cook, stirring constantly, until the noodles are heated through and evenly colored. Add the scallions and stir until well incorporated, about 30 seconds. Transfer to a serving dish. May be served hot or cold.

scallion and ginger soft noodles

Quick to prepare and cook, yet rich in flavor, this simple stir-fried noodle makes a perfect side dish to Western food or part of a multi-course Asian meal. It is also versatile and can be served hot or at room temperature. And it heats up beautifully in the microwave—what more can you ask? ■ SERVES 4 TO 6 AS A SIDE DISH

½ pound Chinese wheat or egg noodles, or vermicelli or thin spaghetti

1 tablespoon plus 2 teaspoons oyster sauce

1 tablespoon light soy sauce

½ teaspoon sugar

2 tablespoons canola oil

1 cup thinly sliced scallions

1 tablespoon peeled and finely minced fresh ginger

1 teaspoon sesame oil, if desired

1 In a large pot of boiling water, cook the noodles until a little softer than al dente. Drain, rinse in cold water, and set aside to drain again.

2 In a small bowl, stir together the oyster sauce, soy sauce, and sugar.

3 In a wok or stir-fry pan, heat the canola oil over medium-high heat. When the oil is hot, but not smoking, add the scallions and ginger and cook, stirring, until the scallions turn a darker green, about 1 minute.

4 Sprinkle a few tablespoons of water on the noodles to loosen them, drain, then add them to the pan. Pour the soy sauce mixture over the noodles and stir and toss constantly until the noodles are heated through and evenly colored. Drizzle with sesame oil, if using, and toss a couple of times to distribute evenly. Transfer to a serving platter and serve hot or at room temperature.

five shreds longevity noodles

In Chinese culture, noodles symbolize long life and are served at celebratory occasions such as birthdays and Chinese New Year. My mother used to make homemade noodles for our Chinese birthdays, that is, our birth day based on the lunar calendar. She would joke to us that she'd make them so long we'd have to eat them standing on a step ladder! Today, I rarely have the time to make my own noodles, but good-quality store-bought wheat noodles are still delicious in this dish (even if we eat them sitting only on a chair).

■ SERVES 4 TO 6

12 ounces Chinese wheat or egg noodles, or vermicelli or thin spaghetti

6 medium dried black mushrooms

2 teaspoons cornstarch

2 teaspoons Chinese rice wine or dry sherry

½ pound lean pork, shredded (see page 23), about 1 cup

4 tablespoons oyster sauce

3 tablespoons light soy sauce

2 teaspoons sugar

5 tablespoons canola oil

3 slices unpeeled fresh ginger

2 teaspoons minced garlic

1 medium red bell pepper, cored and shredded

2 cups bean sprouts

4 ounces snow peas, ends snapped off, strings removed and shredded on the diagonal

5 scallions, bulbs split and cut into 1-inch lengths

2 teaspoons sesame oil

1 In a large pot of boiling water, cook the noodles until a little softer than al dente, about 3 minutes. This should take no more than 2 minutes if the noodles are the pre-cooked variety. Drain, rinse in cold water, drain again, and set aside.

2 Soak the mushrooms in hot water for 15 minutes to soften. Drain and squeeze dry, reserving ¼ cup of soaking liquid. With scissors, trim off and discard the woody stems and shred the caps.

3 In a small mixing bowl, whisk the cornstarch and wine together and add the pork. In another bowl, combine the oyster sauce, soy sauce, sugar, and mushroom soaking liquid. Stir until the sugar is dissolved.

4 In a wok, heat 3 tablespoons of the canola oil over high heat. Swirl the oil around the pan and when the oil is hot, but not smoking, toss in the ginger and garlic, and stir them around the pan for a few seconds until fragrant. Stir up the pork again and add it to the pan. Cook, stirring constantly, until the meat separates and is partially cooked, about 1 minute. Add the mushrooms and pepper and cook, stirring, for about 30 seconds. Add the bean sprouts and snow peas and cook, stirring constantly, until the snow peas turn a darker green, about another minute. Remove and discard the ginger, if desired. Transfer to a flat platter.

5 In the same pan, heat the remaining 2 tablespoons of canola oil. Add the noodles and toss for about 1 minute or until heated through. Pour the oyster sauce mixture over the noodles, return the vegetables and meat to the pan and cook, stirring, until the sauce is evenly absorbed into the noodles. Sprinkle with scallions and sesame oil and toss well. Transfer to a platter and serve immediately.

noodles with bean curd sauce

Previously frozen bean curd, with its open, spongy texture works very well in this sauce. It has a firmer texture than fresh bean curd, holds up to stirring and mixing, and soaks up the wonderful bean sauce flavor. Serve the dish with the same vegetable garnish as for Peking Meat-Sauced Noodles (see page 26). ■ SERVES 6

1 pound firm bean curd, previously frozen, or extra-firm bean curd

½ cup plus 2 tablespoons bean paste, preferably Japanese red miso

2 tablespoons hoisin sauce

2 tablespoons dark soy sauce

1 tablespoon sugar

1 pound Chinese wheat or egg noodles, or thin spaghetti

2 tablespoons canola oil

½ cup finely chopped onion

2 teaspoons peeled and minced fresh ginger

1½ teaspoons minced garlic

½ cup thinly sliced scallions

1 tablespoon cornstarch, dissolved in 2 tablespoons water

1 Thaw the bean curd, if frozen, by placing it in a bowl of hot water. When it is completely thawed, gently squeeze out the excess water and cut the cake into ½-inch or smaller cubes.

2 In a small bowl, blend together the bean paste, hoisin sauce, soy sauce, and sugar.

3 In a large pot, bring 5 quarts of water to a boil. Stir the noodles into the boiling water and cook until a little more tender than al dente.

4 While the noodles are cooking, heat the oil in a wok or stir-fry pan over high heat until hot, but not smoking; test by dipping a piece of onion into the oil; it should sizzle. Add the onion to the hot oil and cook, stirring, for about 1 minute. Add the ginger and garlic and stir for 30 seconds. Add the scallions and cook, stirring, until they wilt. Stir in the bean curd and mix a few times. Add the bean paste mixture and 1½ cups water. Blend well with the spatula. Reduce the heat to medium and simmer for about 1 minute. Pour in the cornstarch mixture and stir constantly until the sauce thickens.

5 Drain the noodles, rinse with hot water, and divide among 6 individual noodle bowls. Serve the bean sauce and vegetable garnish in separate bowls alongside the noodles and let people help themselves to sauce and garnish.

Note: Bean paste, depending upon the brand, can be very salty; a little bit goes a long way. In step 5, start by spooning on a small amount of sauce on the noodles, mix and taste, then add more if desired.

wide rice noodles with beef in black bean sauce

Fresh *chow fun* rice sheets are very perishable and not easily available, so I use extra-wide dried rice noodles from Thailand. They are just as tasty, cook up fast, and store well for that last-minute dish. ■ SERVES 3 TO 4

½ pound extra-wide rice noodles (about ⅜-inch wide)

½ pound flank steak, trimmed

3 tablespoons light soy sauce

2 teaspoons Chinese rice wine or dry sherry

2 teaspoons cornstarch

1 teaspoon sugar

2 tablespoons canola oil

2 teaspoons peeled and minced fresh ginger

2 teaspoons minced garlic

1 medium onion, cut into 1-inch chunks

1 medium red bell pepper, cored and cut into 1-inch chunks

2 scallions, bulbs split and cut into 1-inch pieces

3 tablespoons fermented black beans, rinsed and coarsely chopped

1 In a large pot of boiling water, cook the noodles for 1 minute, then turn off the heat and let the noodles sit in the hot water until soft, about 5 minutes. Drain and rinse in cold water. Set aside to drain again.

2 Cut the meat with the grain into long strips about 2 inches wide. Then slice the long pieces against the grain into ⅛-inch thick slices. In a mixing bowl, whisk together 1 tablespoon of the soy sauce with the wine, cornstarch, and sugar. Add the beef and mix well.

3 In a wok or stir-fry pan, heat the oil over medium-high heat until hot, but not smoking. Add the ginger and garlic and when they begin to sizzle, stir with a spatula for 30 seconds or until fragrant. Be careful not to let the garlic burn or it will be bitter. Add the onion and stir briskly until the onion begins to turn translucent, about 1 minute. Stir up the beef mixture again and add to the pan, cook, stirring, until the beef is partially cooked, about 2 minutes. Add the peppers and scallions and cook, stirring constantly, for another minute, then add the black beans. Continue to stir until well mixed and the scallions turn a darker green, about 1 minute.

4 Sprinkle the noodles with a few tablespoons of tap water to loosen, drain, then add the noodles to the pan with the remaining 2 tablespoons of soy sauce. Cook, stirring constantly, until all the ingredients are well incorporated and the noodles are heated through and evenly colored, 1 to 2 minutes. Transfer to a platter and serve immediately.

stir-fried rice vermicelli with shredded chicken and vegetables

This is a great summer noodle dish. Since rice noodles need only be soaked in hot water, you won't have to heat up the kitchen with boiling water. This dish cooks up quickly, is delicious hot or warm, stores well, and reheats beautifully in the microwave. ■ SERVES 3 TO 4

12 ounces rice vermicelli (phò) or rice sticks

1 teaspoon Chinese rice wine or dry sherry plus 1 tablespoon for the sauce

1 teaspoon light soy sauce

½ teaspoon sesame oil plus 1 tablespoon for garnish

1 teaspoon cornstarch

8 ounces skinless, boneless chicken breast, shredded (see page 23), about 1 cup

⅓ cup canned chicken broth

3 tablespoons oyster sauce

1 tablespoon dark soy sauce

1 teaspoon sugar

3 tablespoons canola oil, divided

2 garlic cloves, minced

½ pound napa cabbage, shredded

1 medium carrot, shredded

3 scallions, bulbs split and cut into 2-inch pieces

1 In a large bowl, soak the rice vermicelli in hot tap water until soft, about 20 minutes; drain and set aside to drain again.

2 In a medium mixing bowl, whisk together 1 teaspoon wine, light soy sauce, ½ teaspoon sesame oil, and 1 teaspoon cornstarch. Stir in the chicken and mix until evenly coated.

3 In a separate bowl, mix together the chicken broth, oyster sauce, dark soy sauce, 1 tablespoon wine, and sugar. Stir until the sugar is dissolved.

4 In a wok or stir-fry pan, heat 1 tablespoon of the canola oil over high heat. Add the garlic and stir until it sizzles. Don't let it burn or it will be bitter. Stir up the chicken again and add to the hot pan. Cook, stirring constantly, until the meat turns white and separates, about 2 minutes. Transfer to a plate with a slotted spoon.

5 In the same pan, add the remaining 2 tablespoons canola oil. When the oil is hot, but not smoking, add the cabbage, carrot, scallions, and drained noodles. Stir and toss to blend the ingredients together, about 1 minute, then pour the sauce over the noodles and cook, stirring, until the noodles have absorbed the cooking liquid, another 4 to 5 minutes. Return the chicken to the pan and toss until well mixed, about 30 seconds. Drizzle with sesame oil and give the noodles a couple of big turns with the spatula. Transfer to a platter and serve hot or warm.

rice vermicelli with sichuan preserved vegetable

Sichuan preserved vegetable infuses the noodles with a rich, pungent taste. It's extremely versatile and keeps indefinitely. It's one of my favorite emergency ingredients, so I always keep a can or two on hand for that quick soup, noodle dish, or stir-fry. Rinse off the heavy coating of red chili powder and salt before using to tone down the spiciness and salinity. ■ SERVES 4 TO 5

12 ounces rice vermicelli or rice sticks

⅓ cup canned chicken broth

4 tablespoons oyster sauce

1 tablespoon Chinese rice wine or dry sherry

1 tablespoon dark soy sauce

1 teaspoon sugar

1 cup dried black mushrooms (about 1 ounce), soaked in hot water for 15 minutes until soft

3 tablespoons canola oil

2 garlic cloves, minced

1 teaspoon peeled and finely minced fresh ginger

½ pound napa cabbage, shredded

1 medium carrot, shredded

4 scallions, bulbs split and cut into 2-inch pieces

½ cup shredded Sichuan preserved vegetable, rinsed and drained

1 tablespoon sesame oil

1 Soak the rice vermicelli in hot tap water for 20 minutes, or until soft. Drain and, holding the noodles up with your fingers, cut them with a pair of scissors, as though you were trimming hair, into shorter lengths for easier stirring.

2 In a small bowl, mix together the broth, oyster sauce, wine, soy sauce, and sugar. Stir until the sugar is dissolved.

3 Drain the mushrooms and squeeze dry. Cut off the stems with scissors and discard. Shred the caps.

4 In a wok or stir-fry pan, heat the canola oil over high heat. Add the garlic and ginger and stir until they sizzle. Add the cabbage, carrot, scallions, Sichuan preserved vegetable, mushrooms, and the drained noodles. Cook, stirring, for about 1 minute, then add the oyster sauce mixture. Cook, stirring, until well mixed, 4 to 5 minutes. Drizzle with sesame oil and give a final two or three big stirs with the spatula. Transfer to a platter and serve hot or warm.

singapore rice sticks

This popular noodle dish has roots in Malay cuisine, and is often served as a quick snack or lunch. The rice sticks, also known as rice vermicelli, absorb the aromatic seasonings and, adding to their convenience, may be easily reheated in the microwave. I prefer to use Madras curry paste for a stronger and more complex curry flavor and aroma. ■ SERVES 4 TO 6

12 ounces rice sticks or rice vermicelli

2 tablespoons and 1 teaspoon light soy sauce, divided

1 teaspoon sesame oil

1 teaspoon Chinese cooking wine or dry sherry

1 teaspoon cornstarch

8 ounces lean pork, shredded, about 1 cup (see page 23)

½ cup canned chicken broth

4 teaspoons Madras curry paste or Madras-style curry powder

1½ teaspoons salt

1 teaspoon sugar

6 medium dried black mushrooms, soaked in hot water for 15 minutes until soft

2 tablespoons canola oil

1 large egg, beaten with ¼ teaspoon salt and ¼ teaspoon dry sherry or Chinese cooking wine

2 slices unpeeled fresh ginger

1 medium onion, shredded

½ pound napa cabbage, shredded (see Note)

1 medium red or green bell pepper, cored and shredded

1 medium carrot, shredded

3 scallions, thinly sliced

1 In a large bowl, soak the rice vermicelli in hot water for 20 minutes or until soft and pliable. Drain and cut with a pair of scissors into shorter lengths so they will be easier to stir.

2 In a small bowl, mix 1 teaspoon of the soy sauce together with the sesame oil, wine, and cornstarch. Stir in the pork and set aside. In another small bowl mix together the broth, curry paste, salt, sugar, and the remaining 2 tablespoons soy sauce.

3 Drain the mushrooms and squeeze dry. Cut off the stems with scissors and discard. Shred the caps.

4 In a wok or stir-fry pan, heat 1 tablespoon canola oil over medium-high heat. When the oil is hot, but not smoking, add the egg mixture and scramble into fine pieces. Remove the eggs from the pan.

5 In the same pan, add the remaining tablespoon of oil and turn the heat to high; do not let the oil smoke. Add the ginger and stir around until it sizzles. Add the pork mixture and cook, stirring constantly, until no pink remains. Add the onion and cook, stirring, for about 30 seconds, then add cabbage, pepper, carrot, scallions, mushrooms, and return the egg to the pan. Cook, stirring, until the cabbage is lightly wilted, 1 to 2 minutes. Sprinkle the noodles with a few tablespoons of tap water to loosen, then add them to the pan. Stir and toss the noodles with two spatulas to combine, then pour in the curry sauce. Cook, stirring, for another 4 to 5 minutes until well mixed and the noodles have absorbed all the liquid. Transfer to a serving platter and serve hot or warm.

Note: You can substitute bean sprouts for the napa cabbage, but because bean sprouts cook quickly, add them to the pan when the noodles go in (in step 5) so they won't overcook.

thai crazy noodles

Why is this dish called "crazy noodles"? I'm told it's because they are so hot and spicy. Since I'm not into spicy food, I like to downgrade the spiciness to something that might be called "sane noodles." But by all means heat the noodles up and go "crazy" by increasing the chili-garlic sauce as much as you want. ■ SERVES 3 TO 4

½ pound wide, flat rice noodles, large ¼-inch width

3 tablespoons oyster sauce

2 tablespoons plus 2 teaspoons dark soy sauce

2 tablespoons white distilled vinegar

1 tablespoon chili-garlic sauce or Sriracha chile sauce, to taste

2 teaspoons fish sauce

2 tablespoons sugar

2 teaspoons Chinese rice wine or dry sherry

2 teaspoons cornstarch

8 ounces lean pork or chicken, thinly sliced (about 1 cup)

3 tablespoons canola oil

2 cloves garlic, sliced

1 small carrot, thinly sliced on the diagonal

5 ounces yu choy or broccoli rabe, cut into 1-inch pieces

½ cup sliced onion

½ cup canned straw mushrooms, drained

6 extra-large raw shrimp (16/20), peeled, deveined, and split in half lengthwise

1 scallion, cut into 2-inch pieces

½ cup fresh Thai basil leaves or sweet basil, packed

¼ cup chopped cilantro (fresh coriander; optional)

1 In a large pot of boiling water, cook the noodles until al dente, about 3 minutes. Don't overcook because they are going to be cooked again. Drain, rinse in cold water, and set aside to drain again.

2 In a small mixing bowl, combine 2 tablespoons of the oyster sauce, the soy sauce, vinegar, chili sauce, fish sauce, and sugar. Stir well to dissolve the sugar. Set aside. In a separate small bowl, whisk together the remaining 2 teaspoons soy sauce, wine, and cornstarch. Add the meat and stir well.

3 In a wok or stir-fry pan, heat the canola oil over medium-high heat; do not let the oil smoke. Add the garlic and cook, stirring, until it sizzles. Be careful not to burn the garlic or it will become bitter. Stir the meat up again and pour it into the pan. Cook, stirring briskly, until the pork is almost cooked, about 2 minutes. Add the carrot, greens, onion, and mushrooms and cook, stirring, until the greens turn a darker color and begin to wilt, about 2 minutes. Stir in the shrimp and cook until the shrimp begins to turn opaque, about 1 minute. Add the noodles and pour the soy sauce mixture over the noodles, loosening the noodles with a pair of chopsticks and stirring until they separate and are heated through and the sauce is well blended.

4 Toss in the scallion and basil and stir until the basil is wilted, about 30 seconds. Transfer to a large serving platter, garnish with cilantro, if using, and serve immediately.

my drunken noodles

There are various stories about the origin for the name of this popular Thai noodle dish. The ones that seem most plausible to me are that eating these noodles can help ameliorate a hangover after too many drinks, or that the spiciness of the noodles causes one to drink a little too much. Either way, with or without alcohol, this noodle dish is delicious. I added water chestnuts to the recipe for a nice crunchy texture, but many different vegetables, such as bell peppers, zucchini, broccoli, baby corn, mushrooms, etc., may be substituted. Adjust the spiciness by simply reducing or increasing the amount of chili-garlic sauce. If you like a very mild amount of heat, like I do, use one teaspoon chili-garlic sauce. ■ SERVES 3 TO 4

½ pound wide, flat rice noodles, large ¼-inch width

4 tablespoons fish sauce

2 tablespoons freshly squeezed lime juice

1 teaspoon to 1 tablespoon chili-garlic sauce, to taste

3 tablespoons light brown sugar

2 teaspoons cornstarch

2 teaspoons Chinese rice wine or dry sherry

8 ounces skinless, boneless chicken breast, thinly sliced (about 1 cup)

3 tablespoons canola oil

2 tablespoons finely minced garlic

1 small onion, cut into ½-inch chunks

1 medium carrot, thinly sliced on the diagonal

3 ounces snow peas, ends snapped, strung, and large ones cut in half on the diagonal

1 cup Thai basil or sweet basil whole leaves, packed

1 In a large pot of boiling water, cook the noodles for about 2 minutes or until al dente. Don't overcook because the noodles will have to be cooked again. Stir occasionally for even cooking. Drain, rinse in cold water, and set aside to drain again.

2 In a small bowl, mix together the fish sauce, lime juice, garlic-chili sauce, and sugar. Stir to dissolve the sugar.

3 In another mixing bowl whisk the cornstarch and wine together. Add the chicken and mix well.

4 Pour the oil into a wok or stir-fry pan and place over medium-high heat. Add the garlic and stir until the oil is hot and the garlic sizzles. Add the onion and the well-stirred chicken mixture and cook, stirring constantly, until the chicken is partially cooked and the onion turns translucent, about 2 minutes. Toss in the carrot and stir another minute. Add the snow peas and basil and stir again until the basil leaves wilt, about 30 seconds.

5 Sprinkle the noodles with a little tap water to loosen them, drain, then add to the pan pouring the fish sauce mixture over them. Cook, stirring constantly, for about 3 minutes or until all the ingredients are well blended and the noodles are heated through. Transfer to a large serving platter and serve immediately.

spicy basil beef noodles

Thai basil has a pronounced anise flavor and the leaves are dark green tinged with purple. If you can't obtain Thai basil, substitute with sweet basil. Instead of snow peas as called for in the recipe, you can use sliced zucchini or bell peppers. ■ SERVES 3 TO 4

---

10 ounces wide, flat rice noodles, medium to extra large width

½ pound beef flank steak, trimmed

3 teaspoons cornstarch

2 teaspoons Chinese rice wine or dry sherry

2 tablespoons oyster sauce

2 tablespoons fish sauce

1 tablespoon dark soy sauce

2 teaspoons chili-garlic sauce

2 teaspoons sugar

3 tablespoons canola oil

2 teaspoons minced garlic

1 cup sliced sweet onions, such as Vidalia

5 ounces snow peas, ends snapped off and strings removed

1 cup loosely packed fresh Thai basil or sweet basil leaves

3 tablespoons chopped cilantro (fresh coriander; optional)

1 In a large pot of boiling water, cook the noodles until pliable, but still firm, about 5 minutes. Drain, rinse in cold water and set aside to drain again.

2 With your knife vertical to the cutting board, cut with the grain along the full length of the meat into long strips, about 2 inches wide. Slice the long pieces against the grain into ⅛-inch thick pieces.

3 In a medium mixing bowl, whisk together the cornstarch and wine, then add the beef and mix thoroughly.

4 In a separate small mixing bowl, combine the oyster sauce, fish sauce, soy sauce, chili sauce, and sugar. Stir to dissolve the sugar.

5 In a wok or stir-fry pan, heat the oil over high heat; do not let the oil smoke. Add the garlic and stir until it sizzles. Add the well-stirred beef mixture and stir a few times to separate, then add the onions and cook, stirring, until the beef is partially cooked, about 2 minutes. Add the snow peas and basil and stir for about 30 seconds. Sprinkle the noodles with a few tablespoons of tap water to loosen, drain, and add it to the pan. Add the oyster sauce mixture and cook, stirring, another minute or so until the meat is done, but not dry. Transfer to a serving platter, garnish with the cilantro if using, and serve immediately.

pad thai

This is one of the most popular noodle dishes in Thailand. I like to make it with a combination of chicken and shrimp. Choose rice noodles that are about ¼ inch wide. ■ SERVES 3 TO 4

½ pound wide, flat rice noodles, medium or large width

12 large shrimp (21/30), shelled and deveined

½ pound skinless, boneless chicken breast, thinly sliced

2 teaspoons cornstarch

5 tablespoons fish sauce

3 tablespoons freshly squeezed lime juice

1 tablespoon ketchup

4 tablespoons sugar

1 teaspoon crushed red pepper, optional

4 tablespoons canola oil

2 tablespoons minced garlic

2 large eggs, beaten

2½ cups fresh bean sprouts

3 scallions, bulbs split and cut into 1-inch pieces

¼ cup unsalted dry-roasted peanuts, chopped

Cilantro sprigs for garnish (optional)

½ lime, cut into wedges

1 Soak the rice noodles in hot water for about 15 minutes or until soft. Drain. In a medium mixing bowl, mix the shrimp and chicken with cornstarch. In a small bowl, mix together the fish sauce, lime juice, ketchup, sugar, and red pepper, if using. Stir until the sugar is dissolved.

2 In a wok or stir-fry pan, heat 2 tablespoons of the oil over medium-high heat until hot, but not smoking. Add the garlic and stir a few times until it sizzles; do not allow the garlic to brown. Stir up the shrimp and chicken mixture and add to the pan, stirring constantly until no pink remains in the chicken, about 3 minutes. Add the fish sauce mixture and stir until mixture comes to a boil. Add the softened rice noodles and stir for about 2 minutes or until the liquid is almost completely absorbed. Remove the noodles to a platter and set aside.

3 Add the remaining 2 tablespoons of oil to the same pan and add the eggs. Let set a few seconds, then lightly scramble, breaking them up into small pieces with a spatula. Return the noodles to the pan and add the bean sprouts and scallions, reserving a small amount of each for garnishing the finished dish. Stir for 30 seconds to mix and transfer the noodles to a plate. Garnish with peanuts, reserved scallions and bean sprouts, and cilantro. Squeeze lime wedges over the top and serve immediately.

bean thread, napa cabbage, and chinese sweet sausage

This is one of my favorite emergency dishes that make a delicious one-dish meal when served with steamed rice. It's quick to cook, my husband loves it, and I always have all the ingredients on hand because they keep so well and are so versatile. Powdered chicken bouillon is a widely used seasoning ingredient with Chinese chefs. It's easy to use if you need only a small amount of chicken broth. It's also economical, readily available, and even a little bit adds an enormous amount of flavor to the dish. A brand popular with Chinese cooks is Lee Kum Kee® Chicken Bouillon Powder. The sausages, which are air-dried, have a pleasantly sweet taste. They keep in the refrigerator for over a month and much longer in the freezer. Both the chicken bouillon powder and Chinese sausages are available in Asian markets. ■ SERVES 2 TO 3

2 ounces bean thread

2 tablespoons canola oil

2 slices unpeeled fresh ginger

2 Chinese sweet sausages, thinly sliced, about ⅛ inch thick

14 ounces napa cabbage

2 teaspoons chicken bouillon powder dissolved in ½ cup water or ½ cup canned chicken broth

1 Soak the bean thread in hot (not boiling) or warm water until soft and flexible. Drain and cut randomly into shorter (about 8-inch) pieces with scissors.

2 Pour the oil in a wok or stir-fry pan and place over high heat. Add the ginger and stir until the oil is hot and the ginger begins to sizzle. Add the sausages and cook, stirring, for about 30 seconds. Add cabbage and broth mixture. Reduce heat to medium-high, stir to mix, and cover. Let steam for about 3 minutes or until cabbage is tender and translucent. Stir occasionally for even cooking. Uncover and add the softened bean thread and stir about 2 minutes or until the noodles turn translucent and absorb most of the liquid. Add salt to taste, especially if not using bouillon powder. Remove and discard the ginger, if desired. Serve immediately.

soup
noodles

homemade chinese chicken broth

Instead of cooking a whole chicken for broth, I freeze bones left over from other dishes. When I have enough saved up, I make my broth. Since Homemade Chinese Chicken Broth is made without salt and is quite light, do not add additional water to the broth as you would when using regular (not low-sodium) canned chicken broth. You can substitute Homemade Chinese Chicken Broth for the canned broth and water called for in the recipes, but add ¼ teaspoon salt to each cup of Chinese Chicken Broth used. When the dish is done, taste and correct the seasoning as needed. ■ MAKES ABOUT 10 CUPS

3 to 4 pounds chicken bones, such as backs, necks, wings, ribs, feet

2 tablespoons Chinese rice wine or dry sherry

4 slices unpeeled fresh ginger

1 scallion

1 Bring a large amount of water to a boil in a stock pot large enough to hold all the bones and enough water to cover them. Blanch the bones by dropping them in the boiling water. When the water returns to a boil, 3 to 5 minutes, drain the bones in a colander and rinse with cold water. This blanching ensures a clearer broth.

2 Rinse and scrub out any clinging scum from the stockpot. Put the chicken bones back into the pot with just enough cold water to cover them. Add the wine, ginger, and scallion, bring the water to a boil over high heat, and immediately turn the heat down to maintain a simmer; do not cover the pot.

3 Simmer, uncovered, for 1½ to 2 hours, or until the chicken is tender and the bones fall apart easily. While the broth cooks, skim off any foam or impurities and discard. Remember, it's the slow simmering that makes a good broth, so don't rush this process.

4 Skim off the fat that is on the surface and remove any large bones. Remove and discard the ginger, if desired. Strain the broth through a fine-mesh strainer or through 2 layers of damp cheesecloth spread over a colander. Cool, uncovered, then refrigerate the broth in a sealed container until ready to use. (Remove any congealed fat before using.) Refrigerated, the stock will keep for about 5 days to 1 week. You may also freeze the broth in 1- or 2-cup containers for easier use.

homemade japanese bonito fish broth (dashi)

This is a basic soup stock that's fundamental to Japanese cuisine. Unlike Chinese and other Asian soup stocks, which are commonly made from chicken or pork bones, this stock gets its flavor from kelp seaweed (*kombu*) and dried tuna (*bonito*). Pieces of tuna are smoked, dried, and fermented and end up looking like pieces of wood. Dried tuna is known as *katsuo-bushi*. It is thinly shaved on a special plane, just like wood, before use. Shaved bonito flakes and kelp seaweed may be purchased in Asian markets and health food stores. If you use homemade dashi, adjust the salt in the recipes to taste. ■ MAKES ABOUT 4 CUPS

5-inch strip of *kombu* (kelp)

1 ounce dried shaved *bonito*—about 3 cups loosely packed

1 Wipe kombu on both sides with damp cloth. Put 4 cups water and kombu in a saucepan over medium heat. When water comes to a boil, remove the kombu and discard.

2 Add shaved bonito to the kombu water and continue to cook until the liquid returns to a boil. Immediately remove from heat and let stand until the bonito settle to the bottom of the pan, 2 to 3 minutes.

3 Skim off any surface foam. Strain liquid through a colander or strainer lined with cheesecloth.

4 Transfer the bonito stock to a bowl and let it cool. Cover tightly and store in the refrigerator until ready to use. Refrigerated, the stock will keep for about 4 days. It may also be frozen for longer storage.

the basic broths

Asian soup noodles most commonly use a soup base of either chicken broth or, in the case of Japanese soup noodles, fish broth. Both of these can be made either from scratch or conveniently from a can or a powder.

CHINESE CHICKEN BROTH: If you have the time and inclination, by all means make your own Chinese chicken broth for the soup noodles. But I have to admit that I do not always have homemade chicken broth on hand, and more often than not substitute canned broth for convenience. Use regular chicken broth, not the low-sodium variety, since you'll be diluting it with water. I like to use either College Inn® or Swanson® brands. I would not recommend canned Chinese chicken broth from Asian markets. I've found that some of them taste very salty and metallic.

JAPANESE FISH BROTH: The Japanese use a fish broth called *dashi*. You can make your own with seaweed and bonito fish flakes or use instant dashi powder, a convenience many Asian households and restaurants use. It's quick, easy, and because it's a powder you can make as much or as little as you need. The brand I prefer is Ajinomoto® Hon-Dashi® bonito fish soup stock.

cantonese roast duck soup noodles

The Cantonese are famous for their delicious roasted and barbecued meats. Purchase a whole or half roast duck in a Chinese barbecue market and be sure to ask them to chop it up. Then with boiled noodles, some greens, roast duck pieces, and piping hot broth—voilà, your meal is ready! Any leftover roast duck will keep in the refrigerator for about a week or in the freezer for longer storage. ■ SERVES 4

12 ounces Chinese wheat or egg noodles, or vermicelli or thin spaghetti

4 cups canned chicken broth plus 4 cups water

2 teaspoons Chinese rice wine or dry sherry

3 slices unpeeled fresh ginger

8 ounces *yu choy*, cut into 2-inch pieces, or other fresh greens such as spinach, watercress napa cabbage, etc.

½ Chinese roast duck, chopped into bite-sized pieces

½ teaspoon salt, or to taste

1 scallion, thinly sliced

1 In a large pot of boiling water, cook the dried noodles until a little softer than al dente, about 3 minutes, or 2 minutes if the noodles are fresh. Drain, rinse in cold water, and set aside to drain again.

2 Pour the broth mixture in a saucepan and add the wine and ginger. Bring to a boil over medium heat. Add the greens and cook until they are just wilted and tender; do not overcook. Add the duck—about 3 to 5 pieces per person—and 2 or 3 tablespoons of the sauce that the shops pack with the duck. Cook until the broth just returns to a boil. Remove from the heat and add salt to taste.

3 Rinse the cooked noodles with a kettle of boiling water to warm and loosen. Drain thoroughly and divide the noodles evenly between four large noodle bowls. Top each bowl with some of the greens, pieces of duck, and a teaspoonful of the scallion. Remove and discard the ginger from the broth, if desired. Ladle the hot broth over the toppings and noodles and serve immediately.

Note: Do not let the noodles sit too long in the hot broth because they will absorb the liquid and lose their chewy texture.

chinese chicken noodle soup

Noodles are most popular in the wheat-growing north of China, but all Chinese enjoy a steaming bowl of noodles as a light meal or midnight snack. In Asia, noodle shops or noodle vendors with their carts are everywhere. ■ SERVES 4

12 ounces Chinese wheat or egg noodles, or thin spaghetti or vermicelli

4 cups canned chicken broth plus 4 cups water

3 slices unpeeled fresh ginger

1 teaspoon salt, or to taste

¼ teaspoon freshly ground white pepper

1 teaspoon cornstarch

1 teaspoon Chinese rice wine or dry sherry

1 pound skinless, boneless chicken breast, shredded (see page 23), about 2 cups

5 cups spinach, watercress, or napa cabbage, cut into 2-inch pieces

2 teaspoons sesame oil, for garnish

1 In a large pot, bring 4 quarts of water to a boil. Add the noodles and cook until a little more tender than al dente. Stir occasionally to keep the noodles from sticking together. When done, drain, rinse thoroughly with cold water, and set aside to drain again.

2 While the noodles are cooking, mix the chicken broth, ginger, salt, and pepper together in a saucepan and heat to boiling.

3 In a small bowl, whisk the cornstarch and wine together and add the chicken. When the broth is boiling, add the well-stirred chicken mixture and cook, stirring constantly, until the chicken shreds are separated and white, about 1 minute. Stir in the greens and cook, stirring, just until wilted; if using napa cabbage, cook until the white parts are translucent, about 2 minutes.

4 When ready to serve, reheat the noodles by rinsing them with a kettle of boiling water or under hot tap water. Drain and divide the noodles among 4 individual bowls. Remove and discard the ginger, if desired. Ladle the hot soup over the noodles and top with pieces of chicken and vegetables. You can also reheat the cold noodles in the soup and then divide them into bowls with the chicken and vegetables, and ladle on the hot broth. Drizzle ½ teaspoon sesame oil into each bowl. Serve hot.

snow cabbage and shredded chicken soup with noodles

The leafy greens and stems of a mustard family vegetable are pickled in brine and chopped for a handy ingredient. It is especially popular in the Chinese provinces of *Zhejiang* and *Jiangsu*, where it's known poetically as "Red-in-Snow." The name comes from the fact that the roots are red and often sprout in early spring through the snow. My father was from *Zhejiang* province and my mother grew up in *Jiangsu* province, so it's no wonder that cans of snow cabbage were always kept in the pantry. ■ SERVES 3 TO 4

½ pound Chinese wheat or egg noodles, or vermicelli or thin spaghetti

1 teaspoon Chinese rice wine or dry sherry

1 teaspoon cornstarch

¼ pound skinless, boneless chicken breast, shredded (see page 23), about ½ cup

1 tablespoon canola oil

1 slice unpeeled fresh ginger

½ cup canned shredded bamboo shoots, drained

½ cup snow cabbage, drained (see Note)

2 cups canned chicken broth plus 2½ cups water

Salt

1 In a large pot, bring 3 quarts of water to a boil. Add the noodles and cook until a little more tender than al dente, but not soft. Stir occasionally to keep the noodles from sticking together. When done, drain, rinse thoroughly with cold water, and drain well.

2 While the noodles are cooking, mix the wine and cornstarch in a small bowl. Add the chicken and mix well.

3 In a wok or stir-fry pan, heat the oil over medium-high heat until hot, but not smoking. Add the ginger and stir until it becomes fragrant. Stir up the chicken mixture again. Add the well-stirred chicken mixture and cook until the meat turns white, about 1 minute. Add the bamboo shoots and snow cabbage, stir about 30 seconds, and pour in the chicken broth. Bring the soup to a boil. Taste and add salt if desired. Remove and discard the ginger, if desired.

4 Add the noodles to the boiling soup and cook just until they are heated through. Divide the noodles evenly among individual soup bowls. Ladle the soup with pieces of meat and vegetable into each bowl. There should be enough soup to come up to the level of the noodles, but not submerge them. Serve hot.

Note: Snow cabbage is available in cans at Asian markets. The brand I prefer to use is Ma Ling brand pickled cabbage from China.

■ VARIATION: Substitute shredded lean pork for the chicken as well as thin dried rice noodles—also called rice sticks—for the wheat noodles. Soak the rice sticks in warm water until they are tender, then add then to the boiling broth in step 3 and heat through.

traditional pork wontons

Enjoyed throughout China, wontons are little boiled dumplings that, like soup noodles, are enjoyed at breakfast, lunch, or as an anytime snack. The versatile wonton may be served boiled, in soup or, the way many Westerners like them, deep-fried in hot oil. ■ MAKES ABOUT 40 TO 50 WONTONS

5 ounces ground lean pork

3 ounces raw shrimp, shelled, deveined, and finely minced

3 small dried black mushrooms, soaked in hot water 15 minutes until soft, stems cut off and caps finely minced

2 teaspoons finely minced scallion

1 teaspoon cornstarch

1 tablespoon plus 1 teaspoon light soy sauce

1 tablespoon water

1 teaspoon Chinese rice wine or dry sherry

1 pound square wonton skins

1 Combine all the ingredients except the wonton skins in a bowl. Stir together until well mixed.

2 With the tip of a table knife, place ½ to 1 teaspoonful of meat mixture in the center of a wonton skin. Fold the skin in half, edge to edge, over the filling to form a rectangle. Fold in half again so the bottom meets the top edge. Moisten the opposite folded corners with a dab of water and press firmly together. The finished wonton should look like a nurse's cap or tortellini. Or fold the skin in half to form a triangle, lightly moisten the edges and press in a plastic dumpling press. Arrange the formed wonton on a baking tray lightly dusted with cornstarch. Cover with a towel. Repeat until all the filling is used up. As you work, keep the stack of wonton skins covered with a damp towel to keep them from drying out.

(continued)

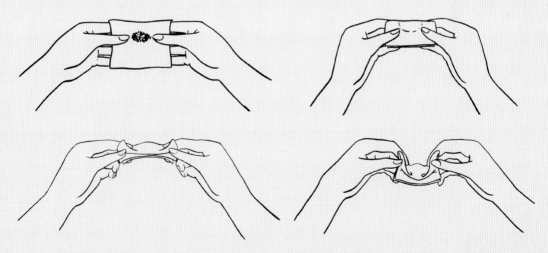

BOILING THE WONTONS: In a large pot, bring 3 quarts of water to a boil over medium heat. Add as many wontons as can swim freely around. Stir gently with a wooden spoon for even cooking. When the water returns to a boil, immediately add 1 cup of cold water. When the water returns to a boil again, remove the pan from the heat, cover, and let the wontons sit in the hot water for 2 to 3 minutes. Be careful not to overcook the wontons or the skins will become too soft and lose their "bite." Scoop out the wontons with a wire strainer and drain well. Serve dry with cider vinegar and soy sauce as a dip or in soup as directed below.

pork wontons in soup as a meal

■ SERVES 4

4 cups canned chicken broth plus 2 cups water

2 slices unpeeled fresh ginger

Salt, to taste

10 spinach leaves or 12 watercress sprigs, cut in half

32 to 48 wontons, boiled and drained according to directions above

2 tablespoons thinly sliced scallion

1 teaspoon sesame oil

1 Bring the chicken broth with the ginger to a boil and add additional salt to taste. Add the spinach leaves and cook until wilted, about 30 seconds. Portion out wontons into individual soup bowls. Sprinkle scallion over the wontons in each bowl.

2 Remove and discard the ginger, if desired. Ladle the hot soup and spinach leaves over the wontons and drizzle with sesame oil. Serve immediately.

turkey wontons

Although pork is traditional in wontons, I've found that ground turkey makes a lower-fat wonton that just as delectable. Boiled or served in soup they make a delicious quick meal, and when fried, perfect appetizers. ■ MAKES ABOUT 50 WONTONS

½ pound ground turkey

⅓ cup frozen chopped spinach, thawed and water squeezed out

¼ cup small shrimp (36/45), finely chopped (about 2 ounces)

1 tablespoon minced scallion

1 teaspoon cornstarch

1 tablespoon plus 1 teaspoon soy sauce, light or dark

1 tablespoon canola oil

1 teaspoon Chinese rice wine or dry sherry

¼ teaspoon salt

1 pound square wonton skins

1 Combine all the ingredients, except the wontons skins in a bowl and stir together until well mixed. Fill and fold the wontons (see page 73). As you work, keep the stack of wonton skins covered with a damp towel to keep them from drying out.

2 Bring 3 quarts of water to a boil in a large pot over medium heat. Add as many wontons as can freely swim about. Stir gently with a wooden spoon and allow the water to return to a boil. Immediately add 1 cup of cold water and when the water returns to a boil again, remove the pan from the heat. Cover and let the wontons sit in the hot water for 2 to 3 minutes. Be careful not to overcook the wontons or the skins will be become too soft and lose their "bite."

3 Remove the wontons with a wire strainer and drain in a colander. Serve hot in soup as below.

turkey wontons in soup as a meal

If the boiled wontons have cooled, heat them in the boiling broth for about 30 seconds, being careful not to overcook them, before serving. ■ SERVES 4

4 cups canned chicken broth plus 2 cups water

1 teaspoon light soy sauce

2 slices unpeeled fresh ginger

½ teaspoon salt, or to taste

4 ounces watercress, washed and cut in half, or washed spinach leaves

32 to 48 boiled and drained wontons

1 teaspoon sesame oil

1 tablespoon thinly sliced scallion

1 Bring chicken broth, soy sauce, and ginger to a boil in a saucepan over medium heat. Taste and add salt, as desired.

2 Add the watercress to the boiling broth and cook until it turns a darker green and wilts, about 1 minute. Remove from heat immediately. Remove and discard the ginger, if desired.

3 Divide the boiled wontons evenly among 4 large bowls. Discard the ginger and ladle the hot soup with the watercress into each bowl. Drizzle sesame oil and sprinkle scallion over each bowl. Serve immediately.

shrimp wontons in soup

Soups for wontons are clear broths with simple seasoning and, if desired, a few leaves of spinach or chopped bok choy. The richness of the dish comes from the wontons themselves. 4 or 5 wontons make a nice first course, while 8 to 12 wontons is a meal. Boiled wontons may also be served alone with a simple dipping sauce of soy sauce, ginger, and hot chile oil or just cider vinegar (which is the way I like them). ■ MAKES ABOUT 50 WONTONS

1 pound shrimp, shelled and deveined

6 canned whole water chestnuts, drained and very finely minced

1 large egg white

2 teaspoons sesame oil

1 teaspoon Chinese rice wine or dry sherry

2 teaspoons cornstarch

1 teaspoon salt

1 pound square wonton skins

1 Rinse the shrimp in cold water, drain well, and squeeze dry in paper towels. Chop the shrimp into a paste. Mix the shrimp with the water chestnuts, egg white, sesame oil, wine, cornstarch, and salt. With your hands, fling the mixture against the inside of a large bowl a few times to increase elasticity.

2 Fill and fold the wontons according to directions on page 73. As you work, keep the stack of wonton skins covered with a damp towel to keep them from drying out.

TO BOIL THE WONTONS: In a large pot over medium heat, bring 3 quarts of water to a boil. Drop in as many wontons as can swim freely about, and stir gently with a wooden spoon. When the water returns to a boil, immediately add 1 cup of cold water. When the water returns to a boil a second time, remove the pan from the heat and cover. Let the wontons sit in the hot water just until the filling is cooked through, about 2 to 3 minutes. Be careful not to overcook the wontons or the skins will become too soft and lose their "bite." Remove wontons from the water with a wire strainer and drain well. Serve dry or in soup.

shrimp wontons in soup as a meal

I like the Sichuan preserved vegetable garnish because it adds a richer flavor to the soup base. ■ SERVES 4

4 cups canned chicken broth plus 2 cups water

2 slices unpeeled fresh ginger

Salt, to taste

32 to 48 boiled shrimp wontons

4 tablespoons thinly sliced scallion

4 tablespoons minced Sichuan preserved vegetable (rinsed first before mincing)

1 sheet nori, folded, cut along the fold lines into 3 pieces, and cut into shreds with scissors

Freshly ground white pepper

1 teaspoon sesame oil

1 In a medium saucepan, bring the chicken broth with the ginger to a boil. Taste and add salt, as desired.

2 Place 8 to 12 boiled wontons in large individual bowls. (If the wontons are not hot, heat them by adding the wontons to the boiling broth. Remove and discard the ginger, if desired, then ladle the wontons along with the hot broth into individual bowls and garnish.) Sprinkle some scallion, Sichuan preserved vegetable, nori, and a pinch of pepper over the wontons in each bowl. Remove and discard the ginger from the soup, if desired, then pour 1½ cups of the boiling soup over the wontons and drizzle with ¼ teaspoon sesame oil. Serve immediately.

hong kong wontons and noodles in soup

This quintessential Cantonese comfort food may be eaten for breakfast, lunch, dinner, or anytime in between. It may seem redundant to serve wontons with noodles, but the combination is delicious and satisfying. ■ SERVES 4

½ pound Chinese wheat or egg noodles, or thin spaghetti

4 cups canned chicken broth plus 2 cups water

1 tablespoon light soy sauce

2 teaspoons Chinese cooking wine or dry sherry

2 slices unpeeled fresh ginger

8 ounces *yu choy*, cut into 2-inch pieces, or other greens such as spinach leaves

20 pork, turkey, or shrimp wontons, boiled and drained (page 74)

2 tablespoons thinly sliced scallions

1 In a large pot of boiling water, cook the noodles until a little softer than al dente. Strain out the noodles, rinse in cold water, and set aside to drain thoroughly. Reserve the hot water for use later.

2 In a medium saucepan, combine the chicken broth, soy sauce, wine, and ginger and bring to a boil. Add the *yu choy* and cook until wilted, but still tender, about 1 minute. Remove from heat immediately. Remove and discard the ginger, if desired.

3 Bring the pot of reserved noodle water back to a boil and reheat the noodles by plunging them into the boiling water. Drain the noodles in a colander and divide them among 4 large bowls. Place 5 wontons over the noodles in each bowl and ladle hot broth into the bowls. Divide the greens evenly among the bowls. Garnish with scallion and serve immediately.

peking hot-and-sour noodle soup

A perennial favorite, soup makes a delicious base for noodles, resulting in a filling and fulfilling lunch or light dinner. ■ SERVES 3 TO 4

½ pound Chinese wheat or egg noodles, or thin spaghetti

⅓ cup shredded lean pork (see page 23), about 2 ounces

2 tablespoons cornstarch

1 teaspoon Chinese rice wine or dry sherry

¼ scant cup dried lily flowers (golden needles, see Note), softened in 2 cups hot water for 15 minutes and drained

¼ scant cup dried wood ears (see Note), soaked in 2 cups hot water for 15 minutes until soft, and drained

¼ heaping cup canned sliced bamboo shoots, drained

2 cups canned chicken broth plus 1½ cups water

1 tablespoon light soy sauce

1 large egg, beaten

2 tablespoons cider vinegar

½ teaspoon freshly ground white pepper, or to taste

Salt, to taste

1 teaspoon sesame oil

1 scallion, thinly sliced

Chopped cilantro, for garnish (optional)

1 In a large pot of boiling water, cook the noodles until a little softer than al dente. Stir a few times to prevent sticking. Drain in a colander and rinse in cold water.

2 In a small mixing bowl, combine the pork with 1 teaspoon cornstarch and the wine. In another small bowl, dissolve the remaining 1 tablespoon and 2 teaspoons cornstarch in ½ cup cold water.

3 Drain, rinse, and squeeze out excess liquid from the lily flowers and wood ears. Cut off the tough stems from the lily flowers and woody pieces from the wood ears, if any. Cut the lily flowers in half crosswise and roughly chop the wood ears into ½-inch pieces.

4 In a medium saucepan, combine the chicken broth and soy sauce and bring to a boil over medium high heat. When the broth comes to a boil, add the well-stirred pork mixture. Cook for 30 seconds, then stir in the lily flowers, wood ears, and bamboo shoots. When the soup returns to a boil add the well-mixed cornstarch mixture, stirring constantly until the soup thickens.

5 Pour a stream of the egg into the hot soup and at the same time stir gently to create fine strands of cooked egg. Remove the pan from the heat immediately and add the vinegar and pepper. Taste and correct seasoning, as desired, then stir in the sesame oil.

6 Plunge the noodles in a pot of boiling water or pour a kettle of boiling water over the noodle to reheat them. Drain thoroughly and divide the noodles evenly among individual large soup bowls. Ladle the hot soup over the noodles, garnish with scallions and cilantro, if using, and serve immediately.

Note: Golden needles are the dried, unopened blossoms of a certain kind of day lily used in vegetarian and northern-style dishes. Wood ears, also known as Black Fungus, Cloud Ears, or Tree Ears, are a kind of black, gelatinous fungus that grows on trees.

shredded pork with sichuan vegetable and noodles in soup

I have found that people who are not adept with chopsticks find soup noodles difficult to eat. The noodles slip off a spoon and a fork won't pick up the soup! Chopsticks and a Chinese porcelain soup spoon are really the best and most efficient tools for eating soup noodles. ■ SERVES 3 TO 4

½ pound Chinese wheat or egg noodles, or thin spaghetti

2 teaspoons cornstarch

2 teaspoons Chinese rice wine or dry sherry

2 teaspoons light soy sauce

½ pound lean pork, shredded, about 1 cup (see page 23)

2 tablespoons canola oil

2 slices unpeeled fresh ginger

½ cup shredded Sichuan vegetable, rinsed and drained

2 cups canned chicken broth plus 2½ cups water

1 teaspoon sesame oil

Salt

1 In a large pot of boiling water, cook the noodles until a little more tender than al dente. Stir a few times to prevent sticking. Be careful not to overcook. Drain in a colander and rinse thoroughly in cold water. Set aside.

2 In a small bowl, whisk together the cornstarch, wine, and soy sauce, then add the pork and stir together until the meat is evenly coated.

3 In a wok or stir-fry pan, heat the canola oil over medium-high heat until hot, but not smoking. Add the ginger and stir until the ginger sizzles. Stir up the pork again, pour it into the pan, and cook for 1 minute, stirring constantly. Add the Sichuan vegetable and cook, stirring, until the pork has changed color and is cooked through, about another minute.

4 Add the chicken broth mixture to the pan. Bring to a boil and stir in the sesame oil. Remove and discard the ginger, if desired. Taste and adjust seasoning, adding salt as desired.

5 When ready to serve, return the soup to a boil and add the noodles. When the noodles are heated through, remove from the heat and divide the noodles, soup, pork, and Sichuan vegetable among individual bowls. Serve immediately.

■ VARIATION: Add 2 cups shredded Chinese cabbage (napa or bok choy) when adding the Sichuan vegetable in step 3. Stir until cabbage is wilted. Add the chicken broth and proceed as directed.

egg clouds and tomato noodle soup

Fine egg threads float like clouds among thin somen noodles in this comforting, soothing, and warming dish. The ingredients are simple and inexpensive. Try it as a light lunch or snack. If you can't find somen noodles, use angel hair pasta. ■ SERVES 3 TO 4

2 small tomatoes

½ pound somen noodles or angel hair pasta

4 cups canned chicken broth plus 2 cups water

4 slices unpeeled fresh ginger

2 large eggs

1 teaspoon Chinese rice wine or dry sherry

½ teaspoon salt, or to taste

2 tablespoons thinly sliced scallions

1 In a large pot, bring 3 quarts of water to a boil. With the tip of a paring knife, cut a shallow "x" on the bottom of each tomato. Prepare a bowl of ice water and set aside. Dip the tomatoes in the boiling water for 30 seconds. With a wire strainer, remove the tomatoes and put them immediately into a bowl of ice water to stop the cooking. With a paring knife or your fingers, gently pull the skin off the tomatoes starting at the cross-hatch. Cut the tomatoes into thin wedges.

2 Bring the water used for the tomatoes back to a boil and cook the noodles in the boiling water until a little softer than al dente, about 3 minutes. Drain, rinse in cold water, and set aside in a colander to drain again.

3 In a medium saucepan, combine the chicken broth and ginger and bring to a boil over medium heat.

4 While the broth is coming to a boil, beat the eggs with the wine in a small bowl and set aside.

5 Add the tomatoes to the boiling broth and cook for about 1 minute, stirring a few times. Pour a thin, steady stream of the egg mixture into the broth while stirring gently, but constantly. Add the salt, then taste and correct the seasoning if necessary. Remove and discard the ginger, if desired.

6 Rinse the noodles in hot tap water and drain. Divide the noodles into 4 noodle bowls. Sprinkle scallions over the top and ladle the soup and solids into the bowls. Serve immediately.

watercress and shredded pork noodle soup

Called *xi yang cai* or "foreign vegetable," watercress is an excellent green for soups. Be careful not to overcook it so it maintains its bright green color and fresh, crisp texture. With only a trace of oil, this soup noodle makes a perfect light meal. ■ SERVES 3 TO 4

½ pound Chinese wheat or egg noodles

4 ounces watercress

2 teaspoons Chinese rice wine or dry sherry

2 teaspoons cornstarch

6 ounces lean pork, shredded (about ⅔ cup) (see page 23)

3 cups canned chicken broth plus 3 cups water

2 slices unpeeled fresh ginger

½ teaspoon salt, or to taste

1 In a large pot of boiling water, cook the noodles until a little more tender than al dente. Drain in a colander and rinse under cold water. Set aside to drain again.

2 Wash the watercress and discard any wilted or yellow leaves. Drain and cut the sprigs in half crosswise.

3 In a small mixing bowl, whisk together the wine and cornstarch and mix in the pork.

4 In a medium saucepan over medium-high heat, mix together the chicken broth mixture and ginger. When the broth comes to a boil, mix up the pork again and stir it into the broth. When the broth returns to a boil, add the watercress and cook until the watercress is just wilted, about 30 seconds. Remove from heat immediately. Remove and discard the ginger, if desired. Season with salt to taste.

5 Plunge the noodles in a pot of boiling water for about 30 seconds or pour a kettle of boiling water over the noodles to reheat them. Drain and divide the noodles into 4 individual bowls. Ladle the soup with the pork and watercress over the noodles and serve immediately.

moon-viewing noodles (*tsukimi udon*)

Here's a simple Japanese autumn soup noodle dish traditionally served during the full harvest moon when it is believed that the moon is the brightest. The egg floating in each bowl of noodles is thought to resemble the full moon. The Japanese break a raw egg over the noodles and let the hot broth poach it, keeping the yolk very soft and runny. If you like a firmer yolk, poach the eggs first, then place them on the noodles. ■ SERVES 4

12 ounces udon noodles

2 tablespoons Japanese soy sauce

1 tablespoon mirin (sweet Japanese rice wine)

3 teaspoons of instant dashi powder

4 tablespoons thinly sliced scallions

4 large poached eggs

1 sheet nori, folded in thirds, cut along the fold lines into 3 pieces, and cut into shreds with scissors, optional

1 In a large pot of boiling water, cook the noodles until soft and chewy, about 10 minutes. If using fresh noodles, cook in boiling water about 3 minutes. Test often to avoid overcooking. Drain, rinse in cold water, and set aside to drain again.

2 In a medium saucepan bring 6 cups of water to a boil. Remove from heat and stir in the soy sauce, mirin, and instant dashi powder. Just before serving, plunge the noodles in boiling water for about 30 seconds or pour boiling water over the noodles to reheat them. Drain and divide the noodles among 4 deep noodle bowls. Sprinkle 1 tablespoon scallions into each bowl.

3 Ladle the hot broth over the noodles and carefully place a poached egg in the center of each bowl. Scatter shredded nori, if using, in each bowl and serve immediately.

■ VARIATION: If you substitute soba noodles for the udon noodles, it is known as *tsukimi soba*.

udon noodle casserole with chicken, vegetables, and fish cake (*kamaboko*)

Perfect for a cold-weather meal, this dish is traditionally served in one large or several individual cast-iron or flame-proof ceramic casseroles known as *nabe*, or "cooking pot." You may also serve this dish in separate deep noodle bowls.

Kamaboko is a popular Japanese fish cake used in soups and stews and as a topping in noodle dishes. It is made from assorted white fish that has been pureed, mixed with starch and flavorings, formed into a small loaf or other molded shape, and steamed. Sometimes the outside of the fish cake is colored red or pink. I prefer using the kinds that have no added food coloring. If kamaboko is unavailable, substitute *surimi*, which is sold in supermarkets as artificial crab legs or seafood sticks. ■ SERVES 4

12 ounces udon or soba noodles

4 tablespoons Japanese soy sauce

2 tablespoons mirin (sweet Japanese rice wine)

3 teaspoons instant dashi powder

4 ounces skinless, boneless chicken breast, cut into 1-inch dice

8 medium dried shiitake mushrooms, soaked in hot water until soft, stems removed and caps quartered

1 medium carrot, thinly sliced on the diagonal

3 scallions, bulbs split and cut into 1-inch pieces

8 thin slices of fish cake (*kamaboko*)

4 ounces spinach—blanch in boiling water, rinse in cold water, squeeze out water and cut into 2-inch long pieces

Shichimi tagarashi (Japanese 7-spice powder), for garnish

1 In a pot of boiling water, cook the noodles until a little softer than al dente, or as instructed on the package. Drain the noodles, rinse in cold water, and set aside to drain again.

2 In a medium saucepan, bring 6 cups water to a boil over medium-high heat. Add the soy sauce, mirin, and instant dashi powder. Allow the soup to return to a slow boil, then add the chicken, mushrooms, carrot, scallions, and fish cake. Cook until the chicken is white and cooked through, about 3 minutes. Remove the pan from the heat. If using one large Japanese nabe, this step may be done in the nabe pan.

3 Rinse the noodles in hot tap water and drain. If serving in one large nabe or casserole, then add the noodles and spinach to the casserole. If using individual bowls, divide the noodles among four bowls. Divide the spinach among the bowls, Bring the broth back to a slow boil and ladle the hot broth and ingredients evenly into the bowls. Serve immediately with the Japanese 7-spice powder as a table condiment.

udon in white miso soup with shiitake mushrooms, spinach, and japanese omelette strips

The two commonly used miso are red (*aka*) and white (*shiro*) miso. White miso is lighter in taste than the red, but any kind of miso can be used in this recipe. Instead of spinach use different kinds of greens such as sprigs of watercress or rehydrated *wakame* (seaweed) in the soup. ■ SERVES 4

---

12 ounces udon noodles

2 large eggs

2 tablespoons mirin (sweet Japanese rice wine)

1 teaspoon canola oil

8 medium dried shiitake mushrooms, softened in hot water for 15 minutes

½ cup white miso paste

3 teaspoons instant dashi powder

2 scallions, white and green parts thinly sliced

4 cups spinach leaves, watercress, or 2 tablespoons dried wakame, soaked in cold water for 10 minutes and drained

1 In a large pot of boiling water, cook the noodles until a little softer then al dente, about 3 to 4 minutes for fresh udon or about 10 minutes for dry; do not overcook. Drain and rinse thoroughly in cold water. Set aside to drain again.

2 In a small bowl, beat the eggs with the mirin. With a paper towel, spread the oil over the bottom of a 10- to 12-inch nonstick skillet. Heat over medium heat and when hot add half the egg mixture, tilting the pan back and forth until it covers the bottom of the pan and forms a thin pancake. Cook for about 30 seconds until set and lightly browned. With a thin spatula, flip the egg pancake over and cook the other side for 15 seconds more. Remove from the pan and cook the remaining egg mixture in the same manner. Fold the egg pancakes into thirds and cut into thin strips.

3 Drain the mushrooms and squeeze dry. Cut off the stems with scissors and discard. Shred the caps.

4 In a medium saucepan, bring 6 cups of water to a boil, then turn the heat down to medium. Place the miso in a small bowl, and with a wire whisk blend in ½ cup of the boiling water into the miso paste until smooth. Gradually stir the miso mixture back into the boiling water. Add the instant dashi powder and stir gently until dissolved.

Add the mushrooms; do not allow the liquid to boil again.

5 Plunge the noodles in a pot of boiling water or pour a kettle of boiling water over the noodles to reheat them. Drain and divide into 4 large soup bowls. Divide and scatter the eggs and scallions over the noodles.

6 Add the greens to the soup mixture and cook until just wilted or add the drained wakame, if using, to the soup. Ladle the soup and all the solid ingredients evenly over the bowls and serve immediately.

fox noodles (*kitsune soba*)

Soba is served cold in the summer with a dipping sauce (*zaru soba*) and hot in the winter in fish broth. *Kitsune* means "fox" and the Japanese believe that foxes enjoy eating the fried and seasoned bean curd known as *abura-age*. These are the same thin bean curd pockets used to make *inari-zushi*. Canned or frozen pre-seasoned *abura-age*, available in Asian markets, is ready to use. ■ SERVES 4

---

12 ounces soba noodles

2 tablespoons Japanese soy sauce

1 tablespoon mirin (sweet Japanese rice wine)

3 teaspoons instant dashi powder

12 seasoned bean curd pockets (*abura-age*), cut into ½-inch wide strips

4 tablespoons thinly sliced scallions

1 In a large pot of boiling water, cook the noodles until a little more tender than al dente, 3 to 4 minutes. Stir to keep the noodles from sticking together. Drain, rinse in cold water, and set aside to drain again.

2 In a medium saucepan, bring 6 cups of water to a boil, then remove from the heat and stir in the soy sauce, mirin, and instant dashi powder. Plunge the noodles in a pot of boiling water for 30 seconds or pour a kettle of boiling water over the noodles to reheat them. Drain and divide the noodles among 4 deep noodle bowls. Distribute the bean curd evenly among the bowls and sprinkle 1 tablespoon of the scallions into each bowl.

3 Reheat the broth if necessary until it just comes to a boil. Ladle the hot broth over the noodles and serve immediately.

> ■ VARIATION: For *kitsune udon*, simply substitute udon noodles for the soba noodles.

japanese curry udon

Commonly served in all Japanese noodle shops, often with their own handmade udon noodles, these hefty Japanese wheat noodles are served in a thick curry-flavored broth enriched with vegetables. Some noodle shops have large picture windows facing the street and during mealtime you can watch the chef make these thick, delicious noodles by hand with only a long rolling pin.

Conveniently packaged Japanese curry roux comes in three levels of hotness and is readily available at most Asian markets. The roux is formed into a sectioned slab, much like a chocolate bar. Simply break off what you need. Japanese curry tends to be mild-mannered in the spice arena, so if you like it hot, add some Tabasco sauce or cayenne pepper. ■ SERVES 4

12 ounces udon noodles

1½ tablespoons canola oil

1 small onion, thinly sliced

6 ounces sliced boneless pork or skinless chicken (about 1 cup)

1 medium carrot, cut on the diagonal into ½-inch chunks

1 small potato, peeled and cut into ½-inch chunks

3 teaspoons instant dashi powder mixed into 6 cups water

4 teaspoons Japanese soy sauce

4 teaspoons mirin (sweet Japanese rice wine)

3 to 4 cubes Japanese curry roux, or more to taste (about 1½ ounces)

1 Cook the noodles in a pot of boiling water for 10 to 12 minutes for dey or 3 to 4 minutes for fresh, or until a little softer than al dente. Drain, rinse in cold water, and set aside.

2 In a saucepan, heat the oil over medium heat and sauté the onion until almost translucent, about 2 minutes. Add the pork and continue to stir 1 minute, until almost cooked through. Add the carrot and potato and continue cooking another minute. Add the dashi mixture, soy sauce, and mirin. Bring to a boil and immediately reduce the heat, maintaining a simmer. Cook 4 to 5 minutes or until the vegetables are fork tender.

3 Break the curry roux into small chunks and add them to the broth, stirring until the roux is melted and incorporated into the broth. Increase the heat to medium-high and simmer, stirring constantly, until the broth thickens.

4 Reheat the noodles by either plunging them into a pot of boiling water for about 30 seconds or rinsing them under hot tap water. Drain well and divide noodles into separate bowls. Ladle the soup and ingredients over the noodles. Serve immediately.

Note: If you can't find the Japanese curry roux, substitute 2 tablespoons plus 2 teaspoons of curry powder (or more to taste) and add an additional 3 teaspoons each of the soy sauce and mirin to the broth. Simmer for a few minutes to allow the curry flavor to develop. Dissolve 3 tablespoons of cornstarch in 2 tablespoons of water. Stir in the cornstarch slurry to the simmering soup, stirring constantly, until the soup thickens.

chicken coconut noodle soup

This is a richly flavored noodle soup that is easy to make. Use light coconut milk to cut down on fat and calories if you like. Fresh Thai or serrano chiles, seeded and thinly sliced, are great if you have them, but I usually use chili-garlic sauce because I always have a jar on hand and enjoy its convenience. Increase the chili-garlic sauce if you like your soup fiery hot. ■ SERVES 4

---

12 ounces wide, flat rice noodles, medium width

8 medium dried black mushrooms, soaked in hot water 15 minutes until soft, or 1 cup canned straw mushrooms, drained

4 cups canned chicken broth plus 1 cup water

2 (13½-ounce) cans unsweetened coconut milk

8 ounces skinless, boneless chicken breast, cut into thin strips

5 tablespoons freshly squeezed lime juice

4 tablespoons fish sauce

4 teaspoons chili-garlic sauce, or more to taste

2 tablespoon sugar

20 snow peas, ends snapped off and strings removed and cut on the diagonal into thin shreds, or 8 ounces spinach leaves

6 tablespoons chopped cilantro (fresh coriander)

4 tablespoons thinly sliced scallions

4 sprigs Thai basil or sweet basil

1 Soak the noodles in hot tap water for about 20 minutes, or until soft and pliable. Drain, rinse in cold water, and drain again. Drain the black mushrooms and squeeze dry. Cut off the stems with scissors and discard. Shred the caps.

2 In a medium saucepan, combine the chicken broth mixture, and coconut milk and slowly bring to just boiling over medium-high heat. Cook and stir gently to prevent the coconut milk from curdling. Add the chicken and mushrooms and simmer gently until the chicken is cooked through, about 1 minute.

3 Stir in the lime juice, fish sauce, chili-garlic sauce, and sugar. Remove from the heat.

4 Plunge the noodles in a pot of boiling water and cook, stirring gently to keep the noodles from sticking together, for 1 minute. Drain and immediately portion the noodles into 4 large bowls. Scatter the snow peas, cilantro, scallions, and basil over each bowl. Bring the coconut soup back to a boil. (If using spinach instead of snow peas, add it to the hot soup and cook until wilted, about 30 seconds.) Ladle the hot soup over the noodles, dividing the solid ingredients evenly among the four bowls. Serve immediately.

thai cucumber and mini meatball rice noodle soup

Traditionally the cucumbers are hollowed and stuffed with meat in this dish. In my variation the cucumbers are sliced and the meat made into little meatballs—I found it easier to eat and quicker to make. The taste is just as delicious. This noodle soup should be served immediately after it's ready to prevent the noodles from absorbing too much liquid and the cucumbers from overcooking in the heat of the broth. ■ SERVES 4

½ pound rice vermicelli or rice sticks

5 medium dried black mushrooms, soaked in hot water 15 minutes until soft

½ pound ground lean pork

1 tablespoon cornstarch

1½ teaspoons light brown sugar

½ teaspoon peeled and grated fresh ginger

1 tablespoon and 1 teaspoon light soy sauce

1 tablespoon Chinese rice wine or dry sherry

1 medium cucumber

4 cups canned chicken broth plus 3 cups water

1 tablespoon fish sauce

2 slices unpeeled fresh ginger

1 scallion, thinly sliced on the diagonal

1 Soak the rice vermicelli in hot tap water until flexible and drain. Drain the mushrooms and squeeze dry. Cut off the stems with scissors and discard. Finely mince the caps.

2 In a small bowl, combine the pork, mushrooms, cornstarch, sugar, grated ginger, 1 tablespoon soy sauce, and wine and toss to mix.

3 Partially peel the cucumber by removing most of the skin, but leaving narrow strips of skin down the sides. Trim away the ends and cut the cucumber in half lengthwise. With a teaspoon, scrape away and discard the seeds. Slice the cucumber on the diagonal ¼-inch thick.

4 In a medium saucepan, combine the chicken broth, fish sauce, 1 teaspoon soy sauce, and the slices of ginger. Bring the broth to a boil over medium high heat. Scoop up 1 tablespoon of the meat mixture at a time and form about 20 round balls using your fingertips. Drop the meatballs in the boiling broth one at a time. When the broth returns to a boil, immediately reduce the heat to low and simmer, covered, for 10 minutes. (You can cook the meatballs ahead and keep them warm or reheat them.)

5 When you are ready to serve, bring the broth back to a boil, remove and discard the sliced ginger, if desired, and add the noodles, then the cucumber. Stir 2 or 3 times, remove from the heat, toss in the scallion, and serve immediately.

meatballs with crystal noodle soup

More of a soup than a noodle dish, this recipe makes a satisfying meal in itself, as well as a hearty soup course for as many as 6 as part of a lighter multicourse meal of stir-fried vegetables and bean curd. Add the bean thread only when you're ready to serve. It overcooks easily and can become soft and gluey. ■ SERVES 4

½ pound ground lean pork (1 cup)

1½ teaspoons cornstarch

½ teaspoon salt, or to taste

¼ teaspoon peeled and grated fresh ginger

1 tablespoon light soy sauce

1 teaspoon Chinese rice wine or dry sherry

2 ounces bean thread

2 cups canned chicken broth plus 3 cups water

1 In a mixing bowl, combine the pork with the cornstarch, ¼ teaspoon salt, ginger, soy sauce, and wine. Set aside.

2 Soak the bean thread in warm water for a few minutes until soft. With scissors, cut into shorter lengths. Drain and set aside.

3 In a medium saucepan over medium heat, bring the chicken broth mixture and remaining ¼ teaspoon of salt to a boil. Scoop up 1 tablespoon of the meat mixture at a time and form about 16 to 18 smooth, small balls using your fingertips. Drop the meatballs into the boiling broth. Reduce the heat to low and simmer, covered, until the meatballs are cooked through, about 10 minutes. (You can cook the meatballs ahead and keep them warm or reheat them.) Taste and correct the seasoning as desired. Just before serving, return the broth to a boil and add the bean thread. Stir a few times and serve immediately.

thai hot-and-sour chicken noodle soup

This popular Thai soup, known as *Tom Yum Gai*, is a lively combination of hot, sweet, spicy, and sour. My noodle version is quick and easy, uses readily available ingredients, and has no added fat. The broth is also delicious without the noodles. ■ SERVES 4

---

12 ounces wide, flat rice noodles, medium width

2 teaspoons cornstarch

2 teaspoons Chinese rice wine or dry sherry

12 ounces skinless, boneless chicken breast, thinly sliced

4 cups canned chicken broth plus 2 cups water

3 tablespoons fish sauce

2 tablespoons white vinegar

2 tablespoons freshly squeezed lime juice

2 tablespoons sugar

2 teaspoons crushed red pepper or chili-garlic sauce, or more to taste

Salt, to taste

2 cups fresh bean sprouts

4 tablespoons thinly sliced scallions

4 tablespoons chopped unsalted dry-roasted peanuts

4 tablespoons chopped cilantro (fresh coriander), or more as desired

1 In a large pot of boiling water, cook the noodles until al dente, about 5 minutes. Stir occasionally to keep the noodles from sticking together. Drain, rinse in cold water, and set aside to drain again.

2 In a small mixing bowl, whisk together the cornstarch and wine, then add the chicken and mix well.

3 In a medium saucepan, bring the chicken broth mixture to a boil. Stir in the fish sauce, vinegar, lime juice, sugar, and red pepper.

4 Stir up the chicken again and add to the soup. Stir to separate and cook evenly. When the chicken is white and cooked through, about 1 minute, reduce heat to maintain a simmer. Taste the broth and add salt, if desired.

5 Loosen the noodles by rinsing them in hot tap water. Drain and divide the noodles between 4 large noodle bowls. Garnish each bowl with ½ cup of bean sprouts and 1 tablespoon scallions. Ladle the hot broth along with the chicken into the bowls. Scatter peanuts and cilantro in each bowl and serve immediately with a little dish of chili-garlic sauce for those who want more heat.

vietnamese quick chicken phò

Soul food for the Vietnamese, fine rice noodles are served in a piping hot broth and eaten with garnishes of fresh aromatic herbs. This easy recipe starts with canned chicken broth as the soup base. ■ SERVES 4

12 ounces wide, flat rice noodles, medium width, or rice vermicelli

4 cups canned chicken broth plus 4 cups water

2 tablespoons fish sauce (*nuoc mam*)

3 slices unpeeled fresh ginger

1 cinnamon stick, about 4 inches long

4 whole star anise

12 ounces skinless, boneless chicken breast

4 tablespoons fried shallots (see Note)

2 cups fresh bean sprouts

2 fresh Thai or serrano chile peppers, seeded and thinly sliced

4 ounces fresh cilantro sprigs

4 sprigs fresh mint

4 sprigs Thai basil or regular sweet basil

1 lime, cut into wedges

Chili-garlic sauce, for serving

Hoisin sauce, for serving

1 Soak the rice noodles in hot tap water for 20 minutes. Drain and set aside.

2 In a 2-quart saucepan, combine the chicken broth mixture with the fish sauce, ginger, cinnamon, and star anise. Bring to a boil over medium-high heat. Add the chicken breast and when the broth returns to a boil, reduce heat to maintain a low simmer. Cover and cook 15 minutes, or until the chicken is cooked through. Skim the broth occasionally to remove any foam and fat.

3 When the chicken is done, remove it from the broth. When it is cool enough to handle, tear the meat with your hands into small shreds. Leave the hot broth and spices in the saucepan to develop the flavor fully while shredding the chicken. When ready to serve, drain the broth through a sieve or colander discarding the solids and impurities. Return the broth to the saucepan and bring to a boil.

4 To serve, reheat the noodles by plunging them into a pot of boiling water for about 1 minute, or until tender. Stir with chopsticks to cook evenly. Drain and immediately portion the noodles into individual bowls. Divide the shredded chicken among the bowls and sprinkle 1 tablespoon fried shallots over each, then ladle the hot broth over the noodles. Arrange the fresh garnishes—bean sprouts, chile peppers, cilantro, mint, basil, and lime on a platter and set out on the table. Put chili-garlic sauce and hoisin sauce in small dishes. Allow each diner to garnish his or her own noodles with the herbs and sauces as desired.

Note: To make the crispy fried shallots, thinly slice 3 good-sized shallots. You should have ½ cup. Heat ¼ cup canola oil in a stir-fry pan or skillet over medium heat. When the oil is hot, but not smoking, add the shallots and sauté until golden brown. Remove from the pan and drain on paper towels. Fried shallots or red onions may also be purchased in most Asian markets.

cold
noodles
and noodle
salads

chinese chicken salad with chow mein noodles

It was in Los Angeles back in the 1970s that I tasted my first Chinese chicken salad. Although not a genuine Chinese dish, the combination of Asian flavors with the crispy texture of raw vegetables and American chow mein noodles were addictive. Add the chow mein noodles to the salad just before serving to keep them light and crispy. ■ SERVES 4 TO 6

½ cup rice vinegar

1 tablespoon cider vinegar

2 teaspoons sesame oil

4 teaspoons sugar

½ teaspoon peeled and grated fresh ginger

1 pound skinless, boneless chicken breast, poached, or about 2 cups shredded cooked chicken

4 cups shredded iceberg lettuce

2 cups shredded carrots

¼ cup chopped chives or scallions

1½ cups chow mein noodles

½ cup sliced almonds, toasted

1 In a small bowl or lidded jar, whisk or shake together the rice and cider vinegars, sesame oil, sugar, and ginger. Mix until the sugar is dissolved.

2 Tear the chicken with your hands into tiny shredded pieces. In a large salad bowl, combine the chicken with the lettuce, carrots, and chives. Just before serving, pour the dressing over the salad and toss until thoroughly mixed. Sprinkle with the chow mein noodles and almonds. Serve immediately.

cold noodles with cucumber and chicken shreds

My husband is from New York State and his family recipe for barbecue chicken justifiably came from Cornell University. It's so delicious that we always make a big batch so we always have leftovers. I use this recipe as a great way to use some of that extra chicken. ■ SERVES 4

8 ounces Chinese wheat or egg noodles, or vermicelli

2 cups shredded seedless cucumber

¼ teaspoon salt

1 tablespoon plus 2 teaspoons sesame oil, divided

3 cups fresh bean sprouts

1 scallion, thinly sliced

½ teaspoon peeled and grated fresh ginger

½ teaspoon finely minced garlic

2 teaspoons sugar

⅓ cup canned chicken broth

3 tablespoons light soy sauce

2 tablespoons rice vinegar

1 cup hand-shredded cooked chicken

1 In a pot of boiling water, cook the noodles until a little softer than al dente. While the noodles are cooking, sprinkle the cucumbers with salt, toss, and let stand for 15 minutes to draw out the liquid. Drain and set aside.

2 When the noodles are done, drain, rinse in cold water to remove the starch and drain thoroughly. Toss with 2 teaspoons of the sesame oil to keep the noodles from sticking together.

3 Blanch the bean sprouts in boiling water just long enough to remove the raw taste, about 20 seconds. Drain immediately and run under cold water to stop the cooking. Drain well.

4 In a small bowl, whisk together the scallion, ginger, garlic, sugar, broth, soy sauce, vinegar, and the remaining tablespoon of sesame oil.

5 Transfer the noodles, chicken, bean sprouts, and cucumber to a serving bowl. When ready to serve, pour the soy dressing over the noodles and toss to mix evenly. Taste and add salt as desired.

cold tossed noodles in sesame-ginger vinaigrette

These cold noodles are light and delicious as a warm-weather accompaniment to grilled meats and fish. It's also a snap to prepare. The vinaigrette dressing is excellent on salads too. ■ SERVES 4 AS A SIDE DISH

½ pound Chinese wheat or egg noodles or thin spaghetti

2½ tablespoons rice vinegar

2 tablespoons canola oil

2 tablespoons water

3 teaspoons light soy sauce

2½ teaspoons sugar

2 teaspoons sesame oil

1 garlic clove, lightly crushed with the side of a knife and peeled

½ teaspoon sesame seeds

¼ teaspoon peeled and grated fresh ginger

¼ teaspoon freshly ground black pepper, or to taste

⅛ teaspoon salt, or to taste

2 tablespoons thinly sliced scallions

1 In a large pot, bring 3 quarts of water to a boil. Add the noodles and cook until a little more tender than al dente. Stir occasionally to keep the noodles from sticking together. When done, drain and rinse thoroughly with cold water. Set aside to drain again.

2 In a small bowl, combine the rest of the ingredients, except the scallions. Whisk until well mixed. Pour the dressing and sprinkle the scallions over the noodles and toss well. Cover and let stand for 15 minutes or more before serving so the noodles can absorb the dressing.

spicy peanut sesame noodles

Chinkiang vinegar, named for the city in which it is brewed, is a black vinegar made from glutinous rice and is comparable in taste to balsamic vinegar. Use less of the chili-garlic sauce (or leave it out entirely) for a milder sauce. ■ SERVES 8 AS A SIDE DISH

1 pound Chinese wheat or egg noodles, or thin spaghetti

3 tablespoons sesame oil

3 tablespoons raw sesame seeds

½ cup creamy peanut butter

⅓ cup canned chicken broth, warmed

3 tablespoons light soy sauce

2 tablespoons Chinkiang or balsamic vinegar

1 tablespoon chili-garlic sauce, or to taste

1 teaspoon sugar

3 tablespoons thinly sliced scallions

1 teaspoon peeled and grated fresh ginger

½ seedless cucumber, shredded

¼ pound snow peas, ends snapped off and strings removed, parboiled 15 seconds, drained, rinsed in cold water, and shredded

1 medium carrot, shredded (parboiled 15 seconds and drained, if desired)

¼ cup chopped cilantro (optional)

1 In a large pot, bring 5 quarts of water to a boil and stir in the noodles. Cook until a little more tender than al dente. If you are using fresh Chinese noodles, follow the package directions and be careful not to overcook or the noodles will be mushy. Drain and rinse the noodles under cold water. Drain again and toss with one tablespoon sesame oil, then place the noodles in a large bowl and set aside.

2 Toast the sesame seeds in a small ungreased pan over medium heat. Stir or shake the pan constantly until the sesame seeds turn a light brown. Be careful not to overcook as the seeds burn easily. Transfer the toasted sesame seeds into a *suribachi* (Japanese mortar and wooden pestle) or regular mortar and pestle, reserving 1 tablespoon of the toasted sesame seeds, then crush the rest with the pestle until most of the seeds are broken.

3 In a small bowl, blend the peanut butter with the broth, soy sauce, vinegar, chili-garlic sauce, and sugar into a smooth paste. Stir in the 1 tablespoon of the scallions, the ginger, and crushed sesame seeds. You'll have about 1½ cups of peanut sauce. Cover until ready to use.

4 When ready to serve, gently toss the noodles with the cucumber, snow peas, carrot, peanut sauce, cilantro, if using, and the remaining 2 tablespoons scallions; the best way to avoid breaking the noodles is to use your hands. Transfer the noodles to a serving platter and sprinkle with the reserved sesame seeds.

> ■ VARIATION: Omit the cucumber, snow peas, and carrot, and dress the noodles with ¾ of the peanut sauce, adding more as desired.

cold sesame noodles, sichuan style

Since these noodles are served cold or at room temperature, they are ideal for picnics and potluck meals. Try them sometime instead of the usual potato salad. ■ SERVES 6 TO 8

1 pound Chinese wheat or egg noodles, or thin spaghetti

4 tablespoons sesame oil

1 whole chicken breast (about 1 pound) or about 2 cups shredded, cooked chicken

¼ cup tahini (sesame seed paste)

3 teaspoons finely minced garlic

2 teaspoons peeled and grated fresh ginger

2 teaspoons sugar

1 heaping teaspoon Sichuan peppercorns, toasted and ground (see Note)

3 tablespoons light soy sauce

1 tablespoon rice vinegar

1 tablespoon chile oil

½ cup thinly sliced scallion

3 tablespoons sesame seeds, toasted (see Note)

Cilantro, for garnish (optional)

1 In a large pot, bring 5 quarts of water to a boil and stir in the spaghetti. Cook until a little more tender than al dente; do not overcook or the noodles will be mushy. Drain and rinse under cold water. Drain thoroughly and transfer to a serving platter, not a bowl, and mix in 2 tablespoons of the sesame oil to keep the noodles from sticking together.

2 If using a whole chicken breast, put it in a pot of boiling water. When the water returns to a boil, turn the heat down to a simmer. Simmer, partly covered, until the chicken is cooked through, 20 to 25 minutes. Drain and set out on a plate to cool. When the chicken is cool enough to handle, remove and discard the skin and bones. Shred the meat by hand and spread over the noodles.

3 In a small bowl, blend the sesame seed paste, garlic, ginger, sugar, Sichuan peppercorns, soy sauce, vinegar, chile oil, and the remaining 2 tablespoons of sesame oil to form a thin paste. Pour the sesame paste mixture over the noodles. Reserve 2 tablespoons of scallions and 1 tablespoon of sesame seeds, and sprinkle the remainder over the noodles. Toss together well. I find the best way to get the ingredients evenly mixed is to use my hands. Sprinkle the reserved scallions and sesame seeds over the top of the noodles, then garnish with cilantro and serve. (If making ahead of time, do not garnish. Cover and refrigerate until ready to use. Bring back to room temperature and garnish just before serving.)

Note: Toast the peppercorns in an ungreased skillet over medium heat until they smoke lightly and are fragrant. Don't let them burn. When they are cooled, grind in a mortar with a pestle and sift through a strainer, discarding the larger pieces that do not pass through.

Toast the sesame seeds in an ungreased skillet over medium heat, shaking them constantly until they turn light brown and are fragrant. Watch them carefully because they burn easily. Remove from heat immediately and transfer to a small dish to stop the cooking.

dan dan noodles

Dan Dan Noodles are Sichuan street food at its most traditional. *Dan dan* refers to the thumping sound made by the pails of noodles and sauce at the ends of bamboo panniers as they are carried through the streets in a sort of traveling fast-food restaurant.

The noodles are served cold or tepid. Once assembled, the dish holds well, although the noodles absorb the sauce after an hour. If you like saucier noodles, dress them just before serving. I sometimes add blanched and shredded snow peas or blanched bean sprouts along with the scallions for added texture. ■ SERVES 6 TO 8

---

1 pound Chinese wheat or egg noodles, or thin spaghetti

2 tablespoons sesame oil

¾ cup creamy peanut butter

¾ cup canned chicken broth

2 tablespoons light soy sauce

2 teaspoons chile oil, or to taste

1 heaping teaspoon Sichuan peppercorns, toasted and ground (see page 108)

¼ teaspoon cayenne, or to taste

3 scallions, thinly sliced

1 In a large pot, bring 5 quarts of water to a boil. Add the noodles and cook until a little more tender than al dente. Avoid overcooking, or the noodles will be mushy. Stir occasionally to keep the noodles from sticking together. When done, drain and rinse with cold water until thoroughly cool. Drain well. Transfer to a large serving bowl, and gently toss with 1 tablespoon of the sesame oil (hands work best).

2 In a small bowl, blend the peanut butter and broth together until smooth and creamy. Add the soy sauce, chile oil, the remaining 1 tablespoon of sesame oil, the Sichuan peppercorns, and the cayenne and mix thoroughly. If you have the time, let the sauce sit for 30 minutes or more to allow the spices to develop.

3 Pour the peanut mixture over the cooked noodles, then sprinkle with the scallions and toss. I use my hands to toss the noodles because they mix the ingredients more evenly and the noodles don't break. Serve cool.

> ■ VARIATION: For a vegetable garnish, blanch snow peas and bean sprouts in the boiling water that will be used to cook the noodles. For snow peas, snap off both ends and string ¼ pound of snow peas. Blanch for 10 to 15 seconds. Remove with a wire skimmer and run under cold water to refresh and drain. Cut on the diagonal into shreds. For bean sprouts, blanch 2 cups of bean sprouts in boiling water for 15 seconds. Remove with a wire skimmer and run under cold water. Drain well. Add the vegetables to the noodles with the scallions in step 3.

noodles in garlic-ginger peanut sauce

This is a bold peanut vinaigrette that's bursting with garlic and ginger flavor. It's excellent on either Asian noodles or Italian pasta and is a perfect side dish to almost any grilled fish or meat. If using Italian noodles, I prefer the thinner vermicelli. ■ SERVES 4 TO 6 AS A SIDE DISH

½ pound Chinese wheat or egg noodles, or vermicelli

¼ cup creamy peanut butter

4 tablespoons cider vinegar

1 tablespoon light soy sauce

2 teaspoons sesame oil

3 tablespoons light brown sugar

1 tablespoon peeled and finely minced fresh ginger

1 teaspoon finely minced garlic

2 tablespoons thinly sliced scallions, green part only

1 In a pot of boiling water, cook the noodles until a little softer than al dente. Drain, rinse in cold water, and set aside to drain again.

2 In a small bowl, combine the peanut butter, vinegar, soy sauce, sesame oil, sugar, ginger, and garlic. Stir until smooth.

3 Transfer the noodles to a serving bowl. When ready to serve, pour the peanut dressing over the noodles and toss well. Sprinkle scallions on top and serve at room temperature.

zaru soba

Soba is the Japanese name for buckwheat flour noodles. Zaru is the name for the bamboo trays upon which chilled soba is traditionally served. These thin, brown noodles can be served hot in a broth, but a popular favorite in Japan during the warm summer months is to eat cold soba with a chilled dashi dipping sauce and a dish of condiments to season the sauce just prior to eating. ■ SERVES 4 WITH ½ CUP CHILLED DIPPING SAUCE PER PERSON

2 cups dashi, or 2 cups water plus 1 teaspoon instant dashi powder

½ cup Japanese soy sauce

4 tablespoons mirin (sweet Japanese rice wine)

2 tablespoons sugar

1 pound dried soba noodles

1 sheet nori, folded in thirds, cut along the fold line into 3 pieces, and cut into thin strips (optional)

2 scallions, green and white part thinly sliced

4 tablespoons grated daikon radish (optional)

2 teaspoons prepared wasabi (green horseradish)

2 teaspoons peeled and grated fresh ginger (optional)

1 In a medium saucepan, bring the dashi to a boil, and add in the soy sauce, mirin and sugar. Stir until the sugar is dissolved. Transfer liquid to a bowl, let stand to cool, then cover and store in the refrigerator until well chilled.

2 In a large pot of boiling water, cook the soba noodles until a little softer than al dente, about 3 minutes. Drain in a colander and rinse under cold running water while gently turning and rubbing the noodles between your fingers to rid them of excess starch. Transfer the noodles to a large bowl of iced water and soak until they are well chilled. Drain thoroughly and divide them into four even bundles arranged on a bamboo mat over a plate or plate alone.

3 Sprinkle about 2 tablespoons of nori strips over the top of the noodles and serve with individual cups of dipping sauce and a small dish with the scallion, daikon (if using), wasabi, and ginger condiments.

TO EAT ZARU SOBA: The Japanese like to slurp their noodles noisily. It is not impolite to do so. Add condiments (wasabi, daikon, scallion, ginger) as you wish to your cup of dipping sauce. Mix and with chopsticks pick up some noodles, dip the noodles in the sauce, then eat. My Japanese friends tell me that it is best not to completely submerge the noodles, as they pick up too much sauce, but dip them just up to the top of the noodles. So enjoy and slurp away!

shanghai ginger and scallion cold tossed noodles

Sometimes the simplest dishes are the best. This Shanghai noodle dish gets its flavor from two aromatics—ginger and scallion. Served at room temperature, it makes a great accompaniment to Western food such as grilled fish or fried chicken . . . and no last-minute prep.

■ SERVES 4 AS A SIDE DISH

½ pound Chinese wheat or egg noodles, or thin spaghetti

2 teaspoons sesame oil

2 tablespoons canola oil

1 cup thinly sliced scallions

3 teaspoons peeled and finely minced fresh ginger

¼ cup light soy sauce

1 teaspoon sugar

2 tablespoons chopped cilantro, for garnish (optional)

1 In a large pot, bring 5 quarts of water to a boil and stir in the noodles. Cook until a little more tender than al dente. Drain and rinse under cold water. Drain thoroughly and transfer to a serving dish. Toss the drained noodles with the sesame oil to keep the noodles from sticking together.

2 In a small saucepan, heat the canola oil over medium heat until hot, but not smoking. Add the scallions and ginger and stir for about 15 seconds, or until the scallions turn a darker green and start to wilt. Add the soy sauce and sugar and stir until the sugar has dissolved. Remove from heat and allow to cool.

3 When ready to serve, toss the noodles with the ginger-scallion oil and garnish with reserved cilantro, if using.

japanese summer noodle salad (*hiyashi chuka*)

Traditionally eaten only during the hot summer months, this salad is cooling and very easy to make and assemble. The toppings for the noodles can be almost any combination of shredded ingredients such as blanched snow peas, sliced tomatoes, and leftover cooked meats such as ham, pork or chicken depending upon your taste and what you might have on hand. The vinaigrette can also be used as a salad dressing. Be sure that any ingredients you add are thinly sliced or shredded. ■ SERVES 4 AS A SIDE DISH

½ pound Chinese ramen noodles (*chuka soba*), wheat noodles, or thin spaghetti

6 tablespoons rice vinegar

4 tablespoons water

3 tablespoons Japanese soy sauce

2 tablespoons sugar

3 teaspoons Dijon mustard

2 tablespoons sesame oil

1 Japanese egg omelette (see page 88), shredded

½ cup shredded seedless cucumber

½ cup shredded carrot

1 cup fresh bean sprouts, blanched for 30 seconds, rinsed in cold water, and drained

2 tablespoons toasted sesame seeds (optional, see note, page 108)

Beni shoga (pickled red ginger), for garnish, optional

1 In a pot of boiling water, cook the noodles until a little softer than al dente. Drain, rinse in cold water and set aside to drain again.

2 In a small bowl, combine the vinegar, water, soy sauce, and sugar. Stir until the sugar is dissolved. Whisk in the mustard until it is well incorporated into the dressing. Add the sesame oil and whisk again.

3 Place the noodles in a serving bowl, arrange the shredded Japanese egg omelette, shredded cucumber, shredded carrot, and bean sprouts over the noodles in separate bundles, sprinkle with sesame seeds and *beni shoga*, if using, and dress with the vinaigrette. At the table, toss the noodles and shredded ingredients together and serve.

Note: You may also divide the noodles and toppings among four separate bowls for individual serving.

iced somen noodles

An incredibly light and refreshing hot summer meal that's a classic in Japan. Fine wheat noodles known as somen are served ice cold with a soy dipping sauce flavored with aromatic garnishes. The only cooking to be done is to boil the noodles for about 2 minutes! ■ SERVES 4

10 ounces somen noodles

1½ cups dashi (see page 66), or 1½ cups water plus 1 teaspoon instant dashi powder

½ cup mirin (sweet Japanese rice wine)

½ cup Japanese soy sauce

1 sheet nori, cut into quarters and cut into 2-inch x ⅛-inch wide shreds

4 tablespoons very thinly sliced scallions

2 teaspoons peeled and grated fresh ginger

Ice cubes

1 Untie the bundles of somen noodles and add them, one bundle at a time, to a large pot of boiling water over medium high heat. Stir gently. When the water returns to a boil, add 1 cup of cold water and let the water just return to a boil. Remove from the heat; drain and rinse well with cold water to remove the starch. Set aside to drain again. The total cooking time is about 2 to 3 minutes, or just until the noodles are tender. The noodles are very fine, so remove from heat as soon as they are ready and drain immediately.

2 Make the dipping sauce by combining the dashi, mirin, and soy. Mix well and chill in the refrigerator.

3 Place nori, scallions, and ginger in their own separate little dishes. These are the garnishes for the dipping sauce.

4 To serve, put some ice cubes and about ¾ cup cold water in each of 4 individual serving bowls and divide the noodles evenly among the bowls. Pour ½ cup of the dipping sauce into 4 separate cups. Put the remaining dipping sauce in a small pitcher on the table along with the garnishes. Each diner garnishes his or her own dipping sauce to taste with the scallions, ginger, and nori, then takes a small amount of noodles from the ice water and dips it into the sauce before eating. It's easiest to eat this dish with chopsticks. Enjoy yourself. In Japan it is perfectly acceptable—even desirable—to slurp up the noodles noisily.

> ■ VARIATION: Serve the noodles with a topping of finely shredded seedless cucumber and 3 to 4 peeled and poached large shrimp in each noodle bowl.

vietnamese tossed rice noodle salad with stir-fried pork

I like the added flavor and enrichment of the cooked pork. Substitute chicken if you like.

■ SERVES 4

12 ounces rice vermicelli or Chinese rice sticks (phò)

½ pound boneless thin-cut pork chops, thinly sliced

2 teaspoons minced garlic

1 teaspoon cornstarch

¼ teaspoon peeled and grated fresh ginger

¼ teaspoon freshly ground black pepper

3 tablespoons fish sauce (nuoc mam)

2 tablespoons canola oil

3 scallions, thinly sliced

4 cups shredded Romaine or iceberg lettuce

2 cups fresh bean sprouts

1 cup shredded carrots

1 cup shredded seedless cucumbers

¼ cup fresh mint leaves, chopped

¼ cup cilantro, coarsely chopped

¼ cup unsalted dry-roasted peanuts, chopped

2 cups Nuoc Cham Dipping Sauce (recipe follows)

1 Soak the rice vermicelli in hot or warm water for 15 to 20 minutes until soft. Drain and cut randomly with scissors into 3-inch to 4-inch lengths. Drain and plunge the vermicelli in boiling water for 1 to 2 minutes. Stir to prevent noodles from sticking together. Drain immediately and run under cold water to rinse off excess starch. Drain thoroughly and set aside.

2 In a medium bowl, mix the pork with the garlic, cornstarch, ginger, black pepper, and fish sauce. Marinate for at least 15 minutes.

3 In a wok or stir-fry pan, heat the oil over medium-high heat. When the oil is hot, but not smoking, add in the well-mixed pork mixture and cook, stirring, until the meat is cooked through and no pink can be seen. Transfer to a dish.

4 In the same pan over medium-high heat, cook the scallions, stirring, until wilted, about 30 seconds. Remove from the pan.

5 Spread the lettuce over the bottom of a large platter. Spread the vermicelli on top of the lettuce, fluffing it as you place it. Arrange the bean sprouts, carrots, cucumbers, mint, cilantro, and scallion over the vermicelli. Sprinkle the peanuts over the top. Pour one cup of the nuoc cham dipping sauce over the vegetables and serve. Put extra dipping sauce in a bowl with a ladle at the table so guests may add extra sauce as desired.

nuoc cham dipping sauce

An important and basic dipping sauce for the Vietnamese. Use with rice vermicelli salads and Vietnamese spring rolls. If you can't obtain fresh Thai chilies, use 1 teaspoon Vietnamese chili-garlic sauce, or more if you like it really hot. *Nuoc cham* keeps well in a tightly covered container in the refrigerator for 7 days. ■ MAKES 2 CUPS

1 cup water

½ cup sugar

¼ cup plus 1 tablespoon fish sauce

¼ cup lime juice

2 tablespoons rice vinegar

2 garlic cloves, finely minced

2 to 4 fresh Thai chiles, seeded and thinly sliced

In a small bowl, mix the water and sugar, stirring until the sugar dissolves. Add the fish sauce, lime juice, vinegar, garlic, and chiles. Stir well.

Note: If you like your nuoc cham spicy hot, don't remove the seeds from the Thai chiles.

thai beef salad with deep-fried rice sticks

Dry rice vermicelli or bean thread puff up like white clouds when deep-fried in hot oil. Place the wiry raw noodles in a bag before breaking them with your hands, or they will fly every which way. Fry a small handful at a time. They will more than quadruple in volume and frying too many at one time will lead to uneven frying and noodles overflowing your pan. This recipe is also a great way to use leftover steak. Just slice it cold. ■ SERVES 4

1 cup canola oil

2 ounces dried bean thread or rice vermicelli, broken or cut into smaller pieces

½ pound beef flank steak

¼ teaspoon freshly ground black pepper

1 lemongrass heart, very finely sliced

1 scallion, thinly sliced

2 to 4 fresh Thai, serrano, or jalapeño chiles, seeds removed and finely sliced, or 1 teaspoon Vietnamese chili-garlic sauce (If you like a hotter taste, leave in the chile seeds)

1 teaspoon minced garlic (½ teaspoon if chili-garlic sauce is used)

3½ teaspoons sugar

3 tablespoons freshly squeezed lime juice

2 tablespoons fish sauce (nam pla)

1 tablespoon rice vinegar

5 cups lettuce leaves—romaine, green or red leaf, Boston, or Bibb—torn into bite-size pieces

1 small sweet onion, such as Vidalia, or red onion, thinly sliced

½ seedless cucumber, shredded

¼ cup chopped cilantro

10 mint leaves, chopped

1 In a wok or stir-fry pan, heat 1 cup of the oil over medium-high heat to 375°F on a deep-fry or candy thermometer. The oil should be hot, but not smoking. If you don't have a deep-fry thermometer, test the oil with a strand of dry noodle, it should puff up immediately. Fry the noodles in small batches to insure even frying; do not crowd the pan. The noodles will immediately puff up and turn white. With a wire strainer and cooking chopsticks or tongs, scoop out the puffed noodles immediately and toss them into a clean brown paper bag. Shake to help drain away the excess oil. Reserve 3 teaspoons of the cooking oil and discard the rest.

2 Sprinkle the beef on both sides with black pepper. Heat the reserved oil in a heavy-bottomed skillet or frying pan over medium-high heat. When the oil is hot, brown the beef, about 4 minutes on each side for medium-rare. Remove to a plate and set aside to cool.

3 In a small bowl, combine the lemongrass, scallion, chiles, garlic, sugar, lime juice, fish sauce, and rice vinegar. Stir to dissolve the sugar.

4 Slice the beef into 2-inch wide thin slices against the grain. Set aside.

5 Spread the lettuce on a large platter, leaving room for the noodles to be added later, and arrange the beef over the top. Sprinkle the onions and cucumbers over the beef. If not serving immediately, cover and refrigerate. Just before serving, decorate the edges the platter with the fried noodles, garnish with cilantro and mint, and pour the fish sauce dressing evenly over the meat; do not pour the dressing over the fried noodles or they will quickly become soggy.

thai bean thread salad with shrimp

Refreshing and low in fat, but rich in the typical Thai taste combination of hot, sour, salty, and sweet. This salad is good alone as a light meal, or as part of a multicourse meal. Bean thread noodles are made from mung beans and are also known as cellophane or glass noodles. Don't confuse then with thin rice vermicelli. ■ SERVES 4

2 ounces bean thread

20 extra-large shrimp (16/20), shelled and deveined

4 tablespoons freshly squeezed lime juice

4 tablespoons fish sauce (*nam pla*)

2 tablespoons water

1 teaspoon chili-garlic sauce, or more to taste

2 garlic cloves, finely minced

2 tablespoons sugar

1 medium carrot, shredded

½ cup kohlrabi or jicama, peeled and shredded

¼ cup thinly sliced red onion

1 scallion, thinly sliced on the diagonal

¼ cup coarsely chopped cilantro

1 red Thai or Serrano chili, seeded and thinly sliced (optional)

1 Soak the bean thread in boiling water for 3 to 4 minutes or until translucent. Drain and rinse in cold water. With a pair of scissors, cut the noodles randomly to 3 or 4 inches in length. Set aside to drain thoroughly.

2 Plunge the shrimp in 4 cups of boiling water. When the water returns to a boil, turn off the heat and let the shrimp sit in the water until cooked through, about 5 minutes. Drain immediately, run under cold water, and set aside in a colander to drain thoroughly.

3 In a small bowl, mix together the lime juice, fish sauce, water, chili-garlic sauce, garlic, and sugar. Stir until the sugar has dissolved.

4 Compose the salad by placing the bean thread in a rimmed platter, then sprinkle the carrot, kohlrabi, red onion, and scallion over the noodles. Arrange the shrimp over the vegetables, and sprinkle with the cilantro and fresh chile, if using. If not serving right away, cover and refrigerate. Ten minutes before serving, pour the fish sauce dressing over the top.

vietnamese poached shrimp in herbed rice noodle salad

This dish is a cross between a salad and a noodle dish. The thin rice noodles are served cold and topped with fresh vegetables, herbs, and shrimp to provide crunch, extra flavor and fragrance, and protein. Everything is tossed together with the ubiquitous *nuoc cham*, a deliciously sweet and salty fish sauce mixture that figures prominently in Vietnamese cuisine. ■ SERVES 4

10 ounces rice vermicelli or Chinese rice sticks (*phò*)

16 extra-large shrimp (16/20), shelled, deveined, and split in half lengthwise

½ cup sugar dissolved in ½ cup hot water

½ cup fish sauce (*nuoc mam*)

2 tablespoons freshly squeezed lime juice

2 teaspoons chili-garlic sauce, or more to taste

2 cloves garlic, peeled and finely minced (about 2 teaspoons)

4 cups shredded romaine or iceberg lettuce

4 cups fresh bean sprouts

1½ cups shredded carrots

½ cup lightly packed fresh mint leaves, chopped

½ cup cilantro (fresh coriander), coarsely chopped

½ cup lightly packed fresh Thai basil or sweet basil leaves, chopped

½ cup unsalted dry-roasted peanuts, chopped

2 scallions, thinly sliced

1 Soak the rice vermicelli in hot or warm water for 15 to 20 minutes until soft. Drain and plunge vermicelli in boiling water for 1 to 2 minutes. Stir to prevent noodles from sticking together. The noodles should be soft, but still with a pleasant bite. Drain and rinse thoroughly in cold water to rinse off excess starch. Set aside to drain thoroughly.

2 Drop the shrimp in a small pot of boiling water and cook for about 30 seconds or until they turn opaque. Rinse in cold water to stop the cooking and set aside to drain.

3 In a small bowl, combine the sugar water, fish sauce, lime juice, chili-garlic sauce, and garlic. Mix thoroughly and set aside. This is the *nuoc cham* dipping sauce.

4 Set out 4 large noodle bowls. Divide the rice noodles (about 1½ cups for each bowl) among each bowl. Divide the lettuce, bean sprouts, carrots, mint, cilantro, and basil and place over the noodles in each bowl. Place the vegetables and herbs on top of one another, or if the bowls are large enough, arrange in separate little piles over the noodles. Divide the shrimp evenly and scatter them over the 4 bowls of noodles. Divide and sprinkle the peanuts and scallions over each bowl. Pour ¼ cup of the *nuoc cham* sauce in 4 individual small dishes for each diner to pour over their noodles. Put any extra dipping sauce in a small pitcher at the table so extra sauce may be added as desired. When ready to eat, each diner pours the *nuoc cham* over the noodles and tosses everything together before eating.

bean thread and snow pea salad with egg garnish

The versatile bean thread can be used in stir-fries, soups, mixed with shredded vegetables as a filling, or used cold in salads. Make variations of this simple salad by adding thin shreds of baked ham, cooked chicken or pork, or substituting julienne strips of cucumber for the snow peas. ■ SERVES 4 TO 6 AS A SIDE DISH

---

3 ounces bean thread

3 ounces snow peas, ends snapped off and strings removed (about 1 cup)

1 large egg

¼ teaspoon Chinese rice wine or dry sherry

¼ teaspoon salt

1 teaspoon canola oil

2 tablespoons light soy sauce

2 tablespoons rice vinegar

2 teaspoons sesame oil

3 teaspoons sugar

1 Pour boiling water over the bean thread and soak until they are translucent and tender, 3 to 4 minutes. Drain, rinse in cold water, and with a pair of scissors, cut randomly into shorter lengths. Put aside to drain thoroughly.

2 Plunge the snow peas in boiling water for about 10 seconds. Drain and rinse immediately with cold water to stop the cooking. Shred the snow peas on the diagonal.

3 Beat the egg with the wine and salt. In a 10-inch nonstick skillet, heat the canola oil over medium heat, spreading it evenly over the bottom of the pan with a paper towel. Pour the egg mixture into the skillet and tip the pan back and forth to spread the egg into a very thin pancake. Cook until the edges turn light brown and begin to curl; this will take less than a minute. With a spatula, transfer the egg pancake to a cutting board and cut into 4 even strips. Pile the strips on top of one another, turn sideways, and cut across the strips to make short, fine shreds.

4 In a small bowl, whisk together the soy sauce, vinegar, sesame oil, and sugar until the sugar is dissolved.

5 Transfer the bean thread and snow peas to a serving dish. Just before serving, toss the noodles and snow peas with the soy vinaigrette. Scatter the egg strips on top and serve immediately.

index